GRIEF DIALOGUES
The Book

STORIES ON LOVE AND LOSS

May you always
have love in
your heart &
stories to
share!

Elizabeth
Coplan

Elizabeth Coplan
Editor-in-Chief

Gigi Michaels
Managing Editor and Designer

Beth Rahe Balas
Editor

Rachel Delmar
Program Manager

Front cover photography by Gigi Michaels.

Photograph : United in Grief

Standing left to right: Karen Vargas (Advisory Council Member), Elizabeth Coplan (Founder, Author, Playwright) , Susan Johnson (Author), Florrie Munat (Author), Scott Coplan (Board Member)
Seated: Jenny Coates (Author), Paul Boardman (Author)

Grief Dialogues
1107 First Avenue, Suite 907
Seattle, WA 98101

www.griefdialogues.com
www.stories.griefdialogues.com

Grief Dialogues | The Book
Second edition, 2019
ISBN 978-0-692-04036-2

To all the writers in this book,
you are our heroes.

The most beautiful people we have known are those who have known defeat, known suffering, known struggle, known loss, and have found their way out of those depths.

ELISABETH KUBLER-ROSS

CONTENTS

BEFORE

DURING

FOREWORD

I am a hospital ethicist who specializes in death and dying issues in a busy metropolitan area. I'm also the current VP for the Funeral Consumers Alliance National Board, a not-for-profit organization committed to education and advocacy for after death options. I deal with death on a daily basis. I am frequently present when families are told of the death or imminent death of a loved one. At times, that grief, sudden and all enveloping, is simply overwhelming. And at times, even following a prolonged terminal illness, there is shock, disbelief, and numbness. After working in hospitals for over 20 years, I found that when my own mother died at home with hospice, it was weeks before the initial shock shook loose and I was able to really grieve for her loss. I had no special reprieve from the pain due to my occupational contact with the deaths of others.

Wealth, celebrity, strength of body or mind, there is no way to achieve a status that will protect us from the deaths of those we love. Certainly, there is pathological, complicated grief which requires psychological intervention, but I don't believe that there is the opposite – an optimal or "A+" way of grieving that could be emulated or taught as the 'best practices' way to do it. I have learned that grief is as individual as the person experiencing it. In other words, there is no right path to process grief from beginning to end. There is only the way which evolves for each of us. We are both all together in our suffering and yet, alone as we find our own way through. This amazing reality is reflected in this collection of pieces by a diverse group of writers and poets who share their personal experiences.

Elizabeth Coplan, playwright and author, turned her personal losses and grief into art in the groundbreaking play, *The Grief Dialogues*. In sharing her grief, she starts healing conversations, and teaches others, who work with the grieving, a deeper understanding of compassion and empathy. Elizabeth uses theatre in ways that touch the soul much differently than any classroom course could. She does it again with this book by creating a brilliant collection of thoughts, stories, and poems and offering a variety of grief perspectives. In life, we suffer from great disparity, yet we unite in the inescapable fact of our grief. All must lose those we love and find a way to continue on. Grief is a shared human condition that each of us experience at some point in our lives. While each person's grief and pain are unique, they are also universal. Grief is a shared human condition that each of us can identify with and one that is inescapable.

The sharing of such personal, private experiences feels exquisite in each of these offerings. By reading each story and poem, I realize I made new friends with those authors who obviously, through their writing, understand me and my grief.

Finding a line, poem, or sentiment that speaks to your grief provides its own sort of balm, a sense that you are not alone. Others lived in the space where you are now, and their understanding of loss may lead to a new path forward for you. Vanessa Poster's poem *We Danced* does this. Vanessa perfectly portrays the way we sometimes intertwine the happy and the sad in our memories allowing an image of her time with her love to form in our own minds. Alica Forneret likens her grief to swimming in the ocean as a metaphor that is drawn for us in achingly clear descriptions. Ann Lovejoy shares, with simple elegance, the story of her mother's quick passing and the questioning, "I think she just died but I'm not sure," that is so often the refrain of those caring for loved ones at home. Even I have had this initial response, and I've seen death many times over. Ann's honest story describes an important and very human response to this universal experience. Alison Eckels shares the story of her father's death in "Under the Crabapple Trees" as a tragedy told by those who could not intervene. Linda Shadwell Hart shares in "22 Hours" how she and her family did "fearlessly face down the reaper" to allow her husband, Greg, a peaceful death. Her courage in altering the inevitable outcome to one more kind and loving than nature could provide is admirable. Other lessons come from Maureen Geraghty. In *In Response to Stabbings on the MAX*, she reminds us that at times we must embrace and acknowledge that which is still sweet along with the sour.

This collection has many voices and many paths, and shares deeply personal and moving stories of loss, grief, love, and healing. Maureen Geraghty's poem, *Everywhere* gives hope of healing and remembrance of our loved ones in everyday life. Gwen Goodkin, in *The Greatest Gizmo*, sums it all up nicely, but I won't give away the ending. As I read this collection, I felt like I was seeing different parts of myself and my friends, as we've adjusted over time to those we have lost.

When I counsel those dealing with death and grief, I remind them to utilize the three T's for healing. *Time*, which will march on regardless of our desires but offers a salve of its own; *tears* which promote healing as they fall; and *talking* which allows the hurts, the loves, the funnies, all to come out for review. I'm betting that this book will help all of you pass the time, maybe shed a few tears that needed to fall, and start talking about your grief, to continue your own healing.

Karen Smith, LCSW, PhD

PREFACE

The First Year is the Hardest

What better place to reflect on *Grief Dialogues: The Book* than at a friend's beside in the hospital? One never knows what any day will bring, does one? My work day was interrupted by news of a friend falling and heading to the ER in an ambulance. And suddenly, I'm faced with his mortality.

If we could go beyond the gurney where my friend lies, past the instrument panel that is his headboard, through the wall, we'd find a lovely late September evening. We would enjoy the rosy golden light, the birds chattering, the distant rush of traffic; a snapshot end of precious summer in a pleasant neighborhood. After sunset, the nights are now cold, foreshadowing our incipient winter.

The boxy room where I sit in the hospital reveals not one hint of all this. Window shades and curtains are drawn. Walls are lined with soaps, gloves, needle disposal bins, packets and nozzles, gauges and screens. Over the white noise and beeping, I can hear the bustling staff and moans of distressed patients down the hall.

I can't predict the trajectory of my friend's injury any more than I can see through the wall to the tidy suburban landscape outside. And if I were outside the building, I might catch a glimpse of the mountains or the bay, but would have no sense of the wild mysteries beyond. Tunnel vision seems intrinsic to crisis mode.

The instant I got the call that my dear friend had fallen and that EMTs needed to take him to the hospital, I could see only him and the decisions ahead. I didn't care that we sat on the concrete in front of the dentist office where he'd fallen. The fear of losing him pulled hard on the deep roots that connect us.

I organized the book to reflect these levels of awareness. In the first segment, "Before," authors describe the approach, the narrowing of focus, and arrival at the threshold. How, and why, did we get here?

"During" the event, "things get real." Time stands still, we're immersed, nothing exists except that heart tugging reality. We wail, put up walls, claw and fight - or purse our lips and look away. But there's no denying it: mortality has walked in the door. An impossible finality has arrived, and it's brought baggage.

"After" encompasses a long, long time. Eventually, we must unpack that baggage, to internalize and process what has happened. Tears seep into our bones like rain into soil, birthing a slog of mud, but perhaps, sometimes, becoming fertile ground for growth. At some point, grief's scar tissue becomes integral to who we are. We feel different within ourselves and from others, but really, we are part of a collective human experience.

Grief Dialogues' mantra is *Out of Grief Comes Art*. By sharing our experiences, we nurture a resonant, powerful force for healing ourselves and others.

Pull up a chair and read our stories.

Beth Rahe Balas
Editor

INTRODUCTION

The stories and poems in this book describe lost children, dead mothers, long gone fathers, missed siblings and departed friends. There are poems about whales and flowers and wonderings. What it's like to once be a family of five, now a family of two?

In this book you will find previously untold stories that burst from the author and beg to be told. For "there is no greater agony than bearing an untold story inside you." *Maya Angelou, poet, memoirist, and civil rights activist*

Ever since I was a little girl, I loved stories. My mother would read them to me and I'd make up my own. As I grew older, I began seeing a story in every window and on every street. I remember a recent walk down a residential street in San Francisco. The woman sitting on the stoop of her apartment building is talking softly, sharing her story with someone on the other end of the phone line. "In the absence of fact, we are free to speculate," or so says my husband, and I create a story of love and loss…in my head. It is a story based in my own life experiences, one that allows me to fashion a story of loss with memories in my heart and in my head.

Gloria Steinem once said, "Perhaps we share stories in much the same spirit that explorers share maps, hoping to speed each other's journey, but knowing that the journey we make will be our own."

In 2015, I wrote the play *Hospice: A Love Story* to reconcile in my own mind three recent deaths. Writing a play felt therapeutic. I didn't want the details of prose to confuse the dialogue.

After my play won a few awards and stage-performances, I found people, normally reluctant to start a conversation about death, actually started talking about it. The more I shared my story, the more others shared their stories with me.

My personal goal is to give voice to individual grief experiences and explore the situations, relationships, emotions and even logistics in death and grief. The stories are at times heartbreaking, funny and even conventional, but always thought-provoking.

In a bigger sense, Grief Dialogues is an artistic movement to start a new conversation about dying, death, and grief. It invites us to reconsider the rhetoric and stigma around death and grief, with the understanding that death is natural and transcends race, creed, ethnicity, gender, age, or economics. It is the great equalizer. Our vision is to create a compassionate, empathetic environment to share our own stories of death and grief. Our motto, *Out of Grief Comes Art*, emerges in our plays, films, music, visual art, poems and essays that we share with our audiences (live and online).

There are so many people I wish to thank for their contributions to this book. All the authors of course, and the people they lost. Our editor, Beth Rahe Balas, and program assistant Rachel Delmar. My sister Mary Pohlmann, whose artwork inspires my writing. And a huge thank you to Gigi Michaels, who once again helped me see the beauty in a job well done.

In closing I'd like to share this quote from my friend, Dave Cinamon:

"May your grief eventually succumb to joy. Grief is rich compost from which, perhaps, future joy grows best."

Elizabeth

BEFORE

LAUGH AGAIN

Paul Atreides

So many everyday expressions refer to death in different ways. We insert them into our vocabulary because it is a part of life itself.

"My car died right in the middle of the intersection."

"Got in the car to head out to work this morning and the battery was dead as a doornail."

We don't always associate in negative terms, we've found ways to use them in celebration, as well.

"Woo-hoo! Did you see that? She killed out there tonight," praising a performance at a concert.

A loud, cheerful high-five for a team win: "They slaughtered them, ten to zip!"

In excitement, possibly while watching a race, be it political or otherwise, "These two are in a dead heat."

From shock to anger to sadness, sometimes to relief and acceptance. When it comes to death, our emotions run the gamut. Each person must deal with grief in their own way and in their own time. And, whether it's a friend, relative, or beloved pet, we offer our condolences in terms of people's loss.

Sorry for your loss" becomes our go-to response.

But, what if.... What if we view it in the other terms people use for death? "Beloved wife, mother, grandmother, passed away peacefully surrounded by family and friends."

Passed away. Crossed over. Moved on to a better place, another plane of existence.

Through the centuries artists have imagined the dead as winged beings, glowing among the clouds. Humanity created a place of light and love and called it Heaven, we send our pets over the Rainbow Bridge; peaceful places free from pain and strife. And yet we don't deny there is still grief attached. Scientists believe energy doesn't die, it simply changes form. Based on that, for many people we are energy and therefore we can't die. The energy, that which we might call a soul, changes form from the physical body to something we can't see or touch or hear.

Close to three years ago, as I was right in the middle of writing the third installment of "World of Deadheads" series of paranormal humor novels filled with fun-loving ghosts, my niece was killed trying to save a young boy from abuse. I first saw her when she was about six months old and knew by the glint in her eyes she would be a handful. Indeed, she was a pistol. I called her my Wild Child and it's most likely not a secret among the other nieces and nephews that she was my favorite. On the way home from the funeral I decided she had to become a character in the book, salty language and all.

Between relatives and close friends, she was the sixth death in less than a year, followed by six more over the course of the next several months. That was a long year. It seemed no sooner had my wife and I gotten over one when another came to smack us in the face.

After the attack on the World Trade Center in September 2001, I wrote a short play called *Fusion*, now included in The Grief Dialogues production. It's a thoughtful piece – at least I hope so. The characters ask the audience, those attending a nationally televised memorial, what they did wrong? Why did this happen to them? I wanted to address how we deal with grief on a collective basis.

We hold open services. We build memorials, erect statues. But how do we contribute as individuals, besides creating a mound built with bouquets of flowers, stuffed animals, and handwritten signs and placards?

To be honest, most of us usually don't pay much attention to death until it hits us close to home. For instance, the Sandy Hook massacre stunned me as it did everyone else. It struck a major chord around the world. But, for those not directly involved, life went on even as we all tried to make sense at the senseless killing of innocent children. Years later, while the families toured the country sharing their hurt and anger and offering ideas on gun control, the rest of us had pretty much put it out of mind.

Each subsequent mass shooting again brought the country together for a few short days, or perhaps weeks; the 2015 church shooting in Charleston, South Carolina, the 2016 Pulse Nightclub in Orlando, the 2017 church shooting in Sutherland Springs, Texas.

Then, 58 concert-goers were gunned down on the Las Vegas Strip while attending the Route 91 Harvest Festival. The largest mass shooting in U.S. history. And, it hit home. This time, friends, acquaintances, coworkers, and family members were affected. No matter who you met in the community, they either had been there, knew someone who had been shot or killed, or they were part of the emergency response teams having to deal with the carnage. How do you handle the tragedy when it hits that close? What can you do to help comfort those who grieve? What can you offer when, due to where this took place, victims spanned the globe?

Death is no laughing matter. But, Stanford conducted a study to see how well people coped with tragedy and death. Those who could find humor fared much better than those who took a negative view. Now, we know scientists are not happy until a study can be substantiated.

Therefore, a different Stanford team did a second one, which they presented at the 2011 Society for Personality and Social Psychology Humor Pre-conference, and again found that "optimistic joking is the more powerful emotional regulator."

I remember when my maternal grandmother died. In an adjoining room of the funeral home an aunt cracked jokes. In the main room, relatives were appalled at what they viewed as crass behavior. In reality, it was how she processed her emotions.

Obviously, considering most of my fiction is about dead people, the majority of them funny, my view of death is that it's simply a different form of life. The writer's group I belong to joke when introducing me: "He writes dead people." I typically follow that up with, "Yes, but they're funny dead people."

In the midst of dealing with the killing of 17 students and faculty when a kid opened fire at Marjory Stoneman Douglas High School in Parkland Florida, a group of local Las Vegas writers were putting the finishing touches on *Vegas Strong: A Charity Anthology* to commemorate the Route 91 Festival horror. But we wanted to offer stories of hope and life rather than sadness, grief, and loss. It's a collection of stories about Las Vegas which have nothing to do with the tragedy itself. Each one is about a spot in the valley the author finds unusually beautiful, or a fond memory of a particular experience.

My entry, titled "Mary's Zombies," is neither, really. It's about what I would do in the face of the zombie apocalypse. And it's funny. I wanted to bring humor into the mix, to give readers a reason to smile as they thought about Las Vegas.

In the face of death, we need glimmers of light and hope; to let people know it's okay to go on living, to laugh again.

In Response to Stabbings on the MAX

Maureen Geraghty

I could look for sorrow & worry-
They are right around each corner.
I could throw rocks & cuss, damn this world
and the people who live in it,

But today, the swallows are darting about
in an open, sun scorched sky,
dogs are barking & smells of bacon visit from
a next door kitchen.

Some find that lofty, even insensitive
but I'm simply opening my arms wider,
holding close violence & heartache
along with tall strands of lavender & kid laughs.

I'm hoping to fold it all together,
sweeten the sour
and Care so Big
that hate can't fit.

This Kind of Grief
(and postscript)

Kara L C Jones

This kind of grief
is loud, obnoxious,
rude, invasive.
I do not apologize
for my breasts,
heavy with sorrow,
full of milk
for a dead child
who will never drink.

Postscript: Though I am not in the same space/place I was in two decades ago when my son first died, when I first wrote this, I continue to share it as advocacy. Grief is a bodily, emotional, individual, familial, communal thing. It doesn't happen in a vacuum. The death is the death. But the grief piece rolls on out of our broken open hearts and spills over the floors, the house, our other family members, friends, work, community, social meaning making, everything. It's okay.

You don't have to apologize for being affected. But please do remember -- even if you don't believe it now, trust me, believe me -- you do still have creative agency. You have the agency to mourn what is lost *AND* to re-create meaning, new ways of moving through the world, even newly sculpted versions of life in the face of their death, your own mortality, everything we will lose.

Because let's face it. We will lose everything. This is the nature of life and being human. None of us escape groundlessness and loss. But we have so much creative agency in that groundless dance. I swear. Trust me. Even if you can't possibly believe that now.

GRIEF IS LIKE SWIMMING IN THE MIDDLE OF THE OCEAN (AND I HATE THE OCEAN)

Alica Forneret

Grieving can often feel like you're drowning.

Like you were suddenly plucked off of land — out of your normal, everyday life — and dropped head first into the deep blue sea.

When you realize where you are and start swimming, it can be overwhelming to get acclimated. You get tired really fast — because what the f, you've never had to swim this much before. You get stressed — because why the HELL did this just happen to you? You get irritated — because where is everybody else dealing with this shit? And you get to swimming — because (in our society) life doesn't stop just because your mom's did.

Whether you're out there floating around on the sunny days or the stormy ones, grief is always there. Surrounding you. Maybe you've climbed on top of a log feeling the warmth of the sun for the first time in months, and you're only waist deep, letting your legs hang in, supported and stable. Or maybe you're eyebrow deep, wondering if you'll ever come up for air, with your arms — and life, and the world, and socializing — feeling so heavy that you just can't swim right now.

Randomly, over days, weeks, months, years, you're dragged to the bottom of the ocean by a scary af squid that's wrapped you up in it's tentacles and won't let you up for air — someone in your life says, "Aren't you okay yet!? It's been a year!" or your best friend who stops talking to you "because you cry too much" and they just don't know how to help.

And, even when it's not those overwhelmingly scary, horrendous things making it hard to stay above water, you're constantly being nipped on the toes by annoying little fish — a photo you find in a drawer. Or you're being pooped on by a seagull — that dumbass that says, "Don't forget to wish your mom happy Mother's Day this week-end!" when she's dead. Or you're passed by a boat that is just out of range to hear your scream for help — an ill-intentioned but totally ignorant dummy that flips you off in traffic... on the anniversary of your best friend's suicide.

Some days bring a little relief though. A log floats by to grab onto — you find a side hustle or dedicate more time to playing with your kids or you book in a weekend away. The sun peeks out from behind a cloud — a postcard arrives in the mail or a distant relative shoots you a <3 emoji. Or a super cute seal swims by and brightens your days — see: why I try to pet every puppy I pass on the street.

Unfortunately, you can always see some waves and clouds looming in the distance — holidays, anniversaries, death, anniversaries, babies, weddings, funerals (the list goes on) — and brace yourself constantly for them to hit. They seem never-ending, always on the horizon, and the first laps of wave water or the first drops of rain signal the unavoidable pain that's about to turn into hard days or weeks of fighting the elements.

People pretend like you'll find an island one day, or like there's a way you'll suddenly grow wings and fly out of the water (this is about as likely as controlling when you'll cry a year after someone dies). They pretend like you're not in the middle of the ocean, but voluntarily going swimming with the option of getting out to sunbathe on a warm, dry beach. Like you can climb out of these seemingly shallow waves whenever you need to go to work, whenever you need to celebrate someone else's happiness, or whenever you need to "pull it together" for whatever the hell reason there could possibly be to "get over" your loss.

And that misconception — the misunderstanding that grief doesn't envelop and surround us *constantly* from the moment we lose someone, and sometimes even before we lose them — is what you start to fight. Instead of getting out of the water at that non-existent beach, your arms and legs just get stronger; your brain stops obsessing about when a raft is going to drift by; you do what you can to protect yourself against absurd beliefs and misinformed "help".

Thankfully, every once in a while a badass, glittery Lisa Frank dolphin comes along and lets you grab onto their fin for a break from swimming — a friend that shows up out of the blue with Chinese food, four boxes of tissues, and a "whatever you need" attitude; a coworker who puts their arm on your shoulder decades after your dad has passed and offers to let you cry on their shoulder on a Tuesday; or anyone that lets you be you, for a moment or a day or a year, sad or happy, just trying to ride the waves without drowning.

SUPER-DEATH!

Emma Goldman-Sherman

CHARACTERS (2m)

LUKE and EDWARD are 15 year old twins, but their identical-ness is not a casting imperative. LUKE is dying, imminently, so he may be smaller than EDWARD. LUKE is lithe and wiry and agile, able to move about the stage freely doing 15 year old boy things, like trying to climb the walls! LUKE is trying to make his death okay for his brother.

EDWARD, LUKE's twin brother, is concerned with LUKE's impending death and much more weighed down with the gravity of the situation. EDWARD wants LUKE to have the best death possible.

TIME - Now

PLACE - empty stage with sounds of a hospital room, probably EDWARD has a chair.

Ellipses (. . .) mean the character is reaching to articulate the ineffable, a trying and a failing.

Slashes (/) are the signal to interrupt. G-d is spelled that way because I am superstitious, but please pro-nounce as usual.

The lack of punctuation is something I've been playing with in terms of leaving it up to the process and the production. And some lines work many different ways, as statements or questions, bigger or smaller, and I don't want to limit the possibilities.

Although dying, LUKE exists like a superhero until the end. So no gasping, no weakness, and he probably actually wears a SPIDERMAN suit (minus the face-mask) in spite of what EDWARD says. (These are available online for very low cost. A t-shirt version is $8 and could be worn with sweatpants.)

SUPER-DEATH!

(LIGHTS UP on LUKE staring at the audience and seeing the audience very distinctly while EDWARD sits with his head in his hands. LUKE tries to climb the walls, getting himself physically ready for the big trip, by doing all the physical things he used to be able to do like handstands with push ups, etc. When EDWARD faces the audience, he can only see the view outside the hospital. We hear the sounds of the life-beep and a ventilator. THEY speak like 15 year old boys speak when they are healthy and bold - big!)

LUKE I'm dying! We've got like minutes! If you don't let me give it, it's gonna hurt

EDWARD Stop saying that

LUKE But it will! Let me use my superpower - you don't have one

EDWARD So whaaaat

LUKE Like suuuuck you have to let me

EDWARD You think I'm weak

LUKE This is no time to pretend

EDWARD You're not Spiderman dude - You have no super-powers How pretend is that

LUKE Better if I die in my Spidey suit than some rank hospital gown with my ass hanging out

(beat)

EDWARD Why you?

LUKE You mean why not you?

EDWARD We're twins - it coulda been me

LUKE as far as I can see it could be you, and I'm you
staring at me

EDWARD You see me - what you think is you But I see
you and you don't look like me anymore

LUKE Because I look like Spiderman!
(beat) So why not you - you want to know why

EDWARD Don't

LUKE Because I was born first - Because I'm the one
they chose. Do you see them - there they are.

EDWARD Where Outside In the parking lot

LUKE Right There Can't you see them

EDWARD See who

LUKE They want me - They say they chose me - I think
they work for G-d - and G-d wants me first, if there
is a G-d

EDWARD There's no G-d

LUKE Oh there is a G-d but maybe he's confused - Or
G-d's a she who's got the hots for me

EDWARD Don't

LUKE Smile

EDWARD Fuck off

LUKE Want some oxygen I got plenty

EDWARD Stop

LUKE A once in a lifetime deal and you don't want it

EDWARD Your oxygen

LUKE No My Superpower It will save you - please Edward

EDWARD Maybe I don't want to be saved

LUKE Oh you're gonna tough it out - You don't know what death does
You're only 15

EDWARD So are you - And I'm not dying

LUKE I mean what death does to whoever it leaves behind, the mourning part Grieving I don't want to leave you with that

EDWARD But you are leaving

LUKE I wish I didn't have to go

EDWARD I know

LUKE I'm not afraid for me It doesn't matter what death'll do to me I'll be gone

EDWARD Stop saying that

LUKE Stop stopping me - This is not something you can push away - Death comes and life changes - But I got this thing I can give you - To keep you good for the rest of your life - You won't have to feel my death

EDWARD I will feel your death - whenever the trees start to turn in the autumn - I will hear you in my head singing

LUKE AND EDWARD (to a tune they made up together, from The Lorax) "The trees, the trees, the Truffula trees"

EDWARD like some cat in the hat asshole

LUKE Fuck the trees

EDWARD You don't mean that

LUKE Let me do this thing!

EDWARD No

LUKE You won't have to mourn

EDWARD I want to mourn I want the whole school to send me cards with sorrowful messages that I can keep for the rest of my life - like hundreds of sappy cards with pictures the girls draw of hearts and flowers. I want your death to be honored every year until I graduate. I want to get into an Ivy League school based on the responses I evoke in my essay about grieving the loss of my twin brother. I want to grieve

LUKE But you could choose to be the way you are now - able to write a great essay anyway - without ever having to suffer over me

EDWARD Along with like all your other bodily func- tions I think you lost your hearing dude

LUKE Let me do this thing and you'll be clean, cool, soda

EDWARD Soda

LUKE Full of effervescence!

EDWARD What do you not understand Luke

LUKE I feel the same way you do

EDWARD Whuh

LUKE What's that? You losing it already Man you got to be here til I go Don't freak yet I got at least another few minutes

EDWARD I'm here

LUKE So serious

EDWARD Death is serious - And you're right - I have never seen anyone die before - Except on tv and in movies - And you are me - I mean it's like looking at me - in like a lot more decades

LUKE But the Spidey costume is helping doncha think

EDWARD What Spidey costume

LUKE I'm wearing a Spiderman costume It covers all of me so you don't have to see what I look like

EDWARD Uh that's a fail - You are not wearing a Spiderman costume

LUKE Oh Shit I tried These people I'm with they said I was or I could I don't know--

EDWARD What people

LUKE The ones out there watching me - They've been so patient all night but lately not so much - And they keep making all sorts of promises - To get me to come with them

EDWARD You're emaciated and tied up to tubes. You could be thirty or forty or fifty. Definitely older than our parents - who will be right back by the way - Yeah they're freaking out

LUKE I know - Take good care of them - But don't let me leave you with that - like a brick or anything - Like fuck em if they can't take a joke

EDWARD It's not a joke - Your hair's gone - Your bones jut out The tubes and the oxygen - You're on a ventilator Dude I hate looking at you like this

LUKE You won't have to soon

EDWARD Stop - I take it back

LUKE No need Nothing you ever said to me should cause you a moment's regret

EDWARD Not even the time when I / almost broke your collarbone and--

LUKE (tops EDWARD) Nope - Nothing - Ever

EDWARD But what about when I / tried to get you in trouble for taking--

LUKE (tops again, could be in his face, etc) Anything you ever think of ever Anything that makes you wish you had my forgiveness You have it I give it to you freely For every piss-ant stupid-dumb idiot-thing you ever did to me Anything and you have to give me the same

EDWARD Given - Given Forever
(beat)

LUKE (sings) "Spiderman, Spiderman"
(talks) I got superpowers, bro- they keep telling me I do so please let me help you

EDWARD It won't help me to skip grieving - Don't you get that - You wouldn't skip grieving for me

LUKE Then what am I good for - I keep trying to get you to let me do something - Please anything

EDWARD I don't know - Live

LUKE Fuck you

EDWARD Sorry

LUKE You were the best - You were everything - I wouldn't want to live without you

EDWARD Thanks for that one dickhead - I have to live the rest of my life without you - I have to try to want that

LUKE That's why you should let me do the thing

EDWARD The superpower thing

LUKE Then you'll be fine

EDWARD Whatever it is - However you got the power to do it - It's not what I need. I know you want to give me something - I get it - Some strength or power but it's gonna have to be your life - I mean your death - Because not everyone has a brother - Not everyone has a twin - Not everyone has a twin brother who dies when they're fifteen - I'm gonna have that

LUKE This? No, I don't want to leave you with this

EDWARD You have no choice bro

LUKE But they said, they said I could do this thing, this superpower thing

EDWARD (breaks the fourth wall - sees the audience - or lies) Oh oh Them - I see them now - They're all here for you

LUKE Yeah in my Spidey suit - And cause like - we don't like - know anyone - like dead yet - there are some famous people coming to meet me

EDWARD No way, like who

LUKE (whoever a 15 year old boy today would idolize
- who is already dead - put whoever you want, or you
can say this:) Like Jackie Robinson and Tupac

EDWARD No shit, really?

LUKE Really
(beat)

EDWARD You look amazing in your Spidey suit

LUKE I told you bro
(beat) You gotta let me give you the superpower now

EDWARD Okay Luke, I'm ready

(THEY embrace or do something more organic to the
process)

END

ONE FLEETING MOMENT...

Florrie Munat

When I was a nineteen-year-old college sophomore, my older sister succumbed to viral pneumonia after three days of illness. She died at a hospital in Evanston, Illinois, the same hospital where she and I had been born.

At around age ten, I had developed great pride in her, as she dedicated herself to one brilliant accomplishment after another in theatre and dance. The high school music director selected her original composition – with lyrics from a Louis Untermeyer poem – to be performed by 700 choristers at the annual Spring Concert. For her sophomore project at Denison University, she choreographed Leonard Bernstein's "Fancy Free" and taught six non-dancers to perform in it.

At age nineteen, she and her Yale-educated husband were hired to teach modern dance and English respectively at a private high school near our childhood home. At a school-wide assembly she invited the captains of the football team to come on stage and compete against her in various acts of strength. She beat them handily. At Northwestern University, she became the assistant director for a nationally-known stage director and also choreographed Darius Milhaud's surrealistic ballet, "Le Boeuf sur le Toit" for a sold-out audience.

She generously allowed me to share her life at every juncture until I felt that we were co-conspirators and co-achievers. Though when I thought of her life, I saw brilliant shades of red, yellow, and purple. When I thought of mine, I saw gray.

After her divorce and graduation from Northwestern, she bought a theatre school in San Francisco and moved to the West Coast. I flew out to visit her, and our time together was filled with streetcar rides to Chinatown where we bought rum-flavored mooncakes and ate them watching the late show; rides across the Golden Gate Bridge while she cursed her hot-tempered Romanian business partner and where we once stopped to throw her wedding ring into San Francisco Bay; beyond-our-means steak dinners in Sausalito; after-theater chats with summer stock actors; long into-the-night conversations with Larry, her pianist friend whom we afterward dropped off downtown near the gay bars; and runs for cable cars that never waited.

The time I think of most is the car ride we took on our last night together. We put down the top of her Corvair convertible, and though it was forty degrees we plunged up a winding road through patchy fog until we arrived at the top of Twin Peaks. We parked in the radar station lot, and with the top down and the heater going, we watched the fog roll in from the Pacific and spread across the city, extinguishing all but a few of the lights below. Then the fog would pass on, Market Street would light up again, and San Francisco would be visible once more. But then another heavy blanket of fog would roll in and obscure the city – the process repeated itself over and over again, and we watched in silence. At one point the fog grew so thick that it seemed all the lights would disappear. We both involuntarily leaned forward in our seats in anticipation of utter darkness. But just as the last tiny light was about to be extinguished, the fog passed on, the city appeared again, and we sat back. I remember thinking that must be what death was like – to sit powerless while all the lights you could see were snuffed out one by one.

She died the Tuesday before Thanksgiving – the day after her 25th birthday. I was home on college break and had bought her a gift at our local record store: Ralph Vaughan Williams' *Fantasia on a Theme by Thomas Tallis*. I still have it. Her funeral was held the day after Thanksgiving, and on Sunday I returned to Wisconsin to finish the fall term and take final exams.

Although everything was a blur, I got straight A's.

Between Christmas and New Year's, my mother and father and I flew to San Francisco to empty her apartment, to see her friends and theatre colleagues, and to begin our grieving in a very concrete way. My parents were wise to know we needed to do this together. On our last day, I drove her Corvair to the top of Twin Peaks on a clear, bright afternoon. The buildings of downtown appeared in the distance, and closer by I could see every small window in every building. I wondered what it was about San Francisco that made it such an intriguing city. Yet there was a frightening air of stability about it – a permanence that was unreal.

When I returned to college in January, northern Wisconsin was entombed in snow with below-zero temperatures. The sidewalks that crisscrossed campus had become hard-packed snow trails bordered by mounds of more snow. This white frigid landscape seemed perfect.

One night I left my fourth-floor dorm room and began walking down the stairs to the basement cafeteria. The stairwell had a series of windows that looked out over a wooded area.

Filling the windows was an intricate latticework of bare, black branches standing out against a luminescent night sky. A sense of calm and comfort washed over me, as if I'd taken a deep breath after having been underwater for a long time.

For that one brilliant, fleeting moment, I became the trees and the trees became me and the trees were my sister too and it was all as it was meant to be. And it was good. More than good, it was perfect. Everything was one. Everything was part of the infinite.

And I would never lose her.

Look, there she stands
behind our wall,
gazing in at the windows,
looking through the lattice.
Song of Solomon 2:9

A different version of the essay appears in Florrie Munat's memoir, Be Brave: A Wife's Journey Through Caregiving.

WE DANCED

Vanessa Poster

We danced
when we thought you would live.

We were tourists
among the ghosts in Old Town Albuquerque

walking past the crowds
past the Navajo code talkers
past the past.
Toward a song of streets
a quinceañera?
a block party?

Amplified music.
Dehydrated Air.
The night before my niece's wedding.

When we thought you would live
we danced.

33 then 34 then 35 radiation treatments
mouth sores, coughed-up blood
stomach tube, skin the trunk of an oak
morphine and then more
 more
      more
   more
morphine

you were so brave, my love

Standing, swaying, singing with the band.
Even holding onto your walker, you
led me across the floor.

We danced
when we thought you would live.

I picked a flower and twisted it into a curl of my hair.
I picked you, a jewel of a man.
I let you pick me.

Together, we danced.

CROSSING THE RIVER

Susan Johnson

I am sitting at my desk watching the slender line of Georgia O'Keefe's *Road Past The View II* pour like a river out of the frame and over the basket of shells and wood in my office. It is a graceful and organic line that slithers with a sense of coolness on this mid-July day. It is a map I want to follow. In a little over a month, my husband and I will again journey to Santa Fe, New Mexico where nearly two decades ago, we spent a wonderful vacation discovering each other and a special place of spirit in us and around us. We will see ourselves there younger, tanned-bodied, naked, making love by the side of the road, searching for Hopi visions, listening to Joni Mitchell in quiet courtyards, being together. Like finding old clothes in an attic, I expect we will try on those selves again to see if they still fit, journey to the same places, listen to the same music and watch for the same signs in the earth.

We are now in mid-life, in mid-marriage, in mid-choice. We have no map of our future and are not sure we will be together after this journey. We have traveled far apart and though we hold each other in our animal ways, the reed of our trust has snapped and plays a lonely tune. We will go in search of ourselves, and in journeying to a place of our past, will hope to find a map of our future. The river spills out of the frame into the basket of shells and sage and swirls at my feet.

I am floating face down in the deep end of the pool, staring through the water filtered with ninety degree sunlight at the grate at the bottom of the hopper. I am pulled toward it feet first, bubbles from my nose and mouth exhaling, down, deeper and deeper. I touch. Crying under water is difficult. I want to stay there and suck in the light deep within me, go into the grate and under the pool to an underground river and be sucked out to a sea on a journey that will take me somewhere else.

I want this time to be over, this floating time in mid-life, in mid-choice. I can say the words, I can feel the feelings, but I have lived inside my head for three months, experimenting with different futures. Some that were not viable now are. Some that didn't fit, now could. The distance between possible and probable fuzzes. A lifetime is a long time to spend with just one person. A lifetime is a long time to spend.

I want a future of lighter being, not a sentence of sadness. I want a possibility of trust, not a continuation of suspicion. I want to hold and be held in a hammock of security, in a relationship of compassion that is elastic. I don't want surprises.

I am standing in the cool vault of the bank surrounded by numbered drawers holding sacred documents of families. It is quiet and cool. There is only the noise of the roving camera, scoping the room from side to side. I open our drawer and begin the archaeological dig through Titles of homes once owned, through jewelry that once graced my mother's arms, past wills now out of date, to photographs.

They are still there, our lost children. I sigh and touch their cheeks, see their arms still around each other, their mouths open in a yawn, their eyes still closed. They're still there, safe, nestled in plastic, in the strata of our past, little fossilized twins we bore in another life and who lived their own for just minutes. There is no new information here. It is all familiar.

They haven't aged. They will always be who they first were. How lucky for them, I think today, how lucky for them. I can hold them there in that moment forever, never knowing disappointments we would cause them and they us; never knowing sadness beyond this initial and everlasting one. How nice, I thought, that in a sense I can hold them in the palms of my hands, secure, like this, unchanging. They were possibilities that died and never will be.

They were possibilities that died and never will be, for themselves and for us. Each time I see them I have to let them go again. But every so often I do need to just come and touch them, see them holding each other still, safe. I put them back in the drawer and return the drawer to its cool haven. It is only after having touched them again that I can return to the possibilities that present themselves out there for me now. It is only now, having touched that past that I can turn back to think more about the futures that await.

"All at once, a dark form stood in front of the forest on a patch of snow. It was a grizzly, and behind her, two cubs. Suddenly the sow turned and bolted through the trees. A female elk crashed through the timber to the other side of the clearing, stopped, and swung back toward the bear. Within seconds, the grizzly emerged with an elk calf secure in the grip of her jaws. The sow shook the yearling violently by the nape of its neck, threw it down, clamped her claws on its shoulders, and began tearing the flesh from the bones with her teeth. The cow elk, only a few feet away, watched the sow devour her calf. She pawed the earth desperately with her front hooves, but the bear was oblivious. Blood dripped from the sow's muzzle. The cubs stood by their mother, who eventually turned the carcass over to them. Two hours passed. The sow buried the calf for a later meal, she slept on top of the mound with a paw on each cub. It was not until then that the elk crossed the river in retreat."

from "Undressing the Bear," *An Unspoken Hunger: Stories from the Field* by Terry Tempest Williams

DEATH OF A CHILDHOOD

Jennifer Coates

My father committed suicide when I was 11. My parents divorced the year before, at my mother's instigation. Every other weekend, my 8-year-old brother and I were shuttled back and forth between New Haven Connecticut, where we lived with my mother, and Sherman Connecticut, where my father remained in the house he grew up in, the home I'd known until I was 10. My father went missing before one of the weekends we were supposed to go visit, and I was actually relieved, as these weekends entailed watching him drink bourbon while he complained about my mother and sniped with his new wife into the wee hours of the night, and treading carefully with our sullen step-siblings who had taken over our old rooms.

My brother and I were told that my father had gone to a special spot where we used to spend happy times as a family -- the secluded unused pool of family friends surrounded by gracious trees and a sloping lawn. He had taken sleeping pills. My mother told us that my father did this out of love for us, because life ahead was going to be complicated because of his drinking. My father had been fired from his teaching job of 15 years and was going to spend the summer in jail for totaling his car while driving drunk with a New York driver's license illegally obtained after losing his Connecticut license for the same reason. I myself routinely thought I was about to die while driving with my father. He sped along the curvy roads of Connecticut, often on the wrong side of the street, gesticulating with his free hand, which often held a lit cigarette. When cops stopped us, my father would say he'd been distracted because of us kids. That's what made me mad, the dangerous driving something I just accepted, though I didn't like it. I had gotten used to closing my eyes and ducking down on the floor in the back seat, sitting up only as we pulled in to our destination.

For some reason, I pictured my father sitting in his white Jeep Cherokee as rain pelted the front windshield, nothing outside visible, the inside cabin warm and dry for his transition into death. I would imagine what it felt like to be sitting on the leather seat behind the steering wheel, opening the pill bottle, not hard to open in those days before child-proof pill bottles, taking a sip of water, coffee or the bourbon I'd taste on his mustache when he kissed me goodnight, and then swallowing. Did he hesitate or think about the people he wouldn't see again? My mind paints a window of time and personal space free of the clamor of human voices. I saw him alone with himself inside the patter of rain, calm and free.

I was obsessed with death even before my father died. I dreaded going to sleep at night, believing it extremely likely that I might not see the morning. I would lie in bed and look around my dark room saying goodbye to the familiar shadows -- my stuffed animals, my dolls, my dresser, the sliding doors of my closet, our Beagle-Pekingese Lucy at the end of my bed, wondering what it would be like...to not wake up. I assumed it would be dark, deep, infinite. I was fascinated and terrified. I made a full time project of questioning every adult who came into the house about religious beliefs and reflections on life after death. I'd ask for specific details about their particular religions, grilling them on the internal logic, how they could be sure, what one had to do to assure entry into heaven. I talked to people of the Jewish faith, Catholics, Methodists, Christian Scientists, and Episcopalians. Any conversation could be the one that resolved my questions (and there were many), so I was diligent and persistent. My parents for the most part stayed out of it, neither discouraging nor encouraging my inquiry. When I would tell them what I had learned from a particular talk, they would reiterate their firm belief that there is no organized creative force, no God, no continuation of anything after death. Their unwavering conclusion was that we just rot in the ground after we die. I really didn't like that theory and felt I had to find another truth.

After my father died, my quest for answers about death continued. I still lived in continual and abject terror about my impending fate-- this conveyor belt I was moving on, towards this state that I had no proof was anything other than infinite, dark deep nothingness. One friend's religion had so many rules about being "saved" and one's eligibility to enter heaven that I spent more of my time in panic about whether or not I had found salvation than I spent worrying about death itself.

I tried to pray for my father but they told me he was going to burn in hell for committing suicide and there was nothing I could do. I decided my existential uncertainty was better than the anxiety of this particular religion and others I'd heard about and that I'd have to create my own spiritual peace.

My mother fell into her own depression and anxiety after my father died. She started drinking a lot and would forget to pick my brother and I up from friends' houses and at activities. Walking into the apartment from school with friends, I might find her on the floor in a state of undress, or slurring her words with a Bloody Mary in her hand saying she was a just finishing lunch.

My mother said that my father had told her that if she divorced him he would kill himself, and then, of course, he did that very thing. So, I kind of understood that this might be cause for her to be this upset and drinking all the time. It fit in with my childish sense of my father's sadness causing him to drink a lot and then kill himself. My mind accepted sadness as the reason parents had to drink so much. And yet, I worried what would happen to my brother and I if my mother also died, and wished there weren't so many reasons for them to be sad. I didn't want to go live with my aunt and uncle who combed their daughters' hair until they cried, required clothes to be neatly folded bureau drawers instead of shoved in, and who also had rules about making beds and when to get up, even on weekends. Childhood seemed a precarious place. I looked forward to being old enough not to have to worry about where I might have to live if my mother died.

Need For Comfort
(After reading patty donovan's obituary in the seattle times [2011])

Sara J Glerum

After a short battle with cancer at age 59.
At her request, there will be no service.

That's all the notice says. In the flick of a page,
the slam of a book cover, her chapter is over.

In the same way cops get immune to the ravages of crime, I'm building
up my own immunity to the effects of death. Why then, does this
morning's obituary for a woman I just slightly knew make me so sad?

Without a service, I don't know how to grieve.
Without heirs remaining, I don't know whom to console.
Without a god who listens to the least little detail of my prayers,
I have no way to purge my sorrow.
I need my own wagging tongue, my own adjectives
and anecdotes to hold on to recollection—
hold off her disappearance. When I console another,
I am tamping down bumps of fear along my path.

I want the luxury of attaching meaning
to a life. I want to wail in some primordial voice,
or punch a hole right through my kitchen table.
Or shall I cry for me? I have great need for comfort.

IF ONLY

Jocelyn Williams

When I was single, I had an almost two-decade long regret hanging over my head. I was in my mid 20's and waiting tables at a Creole restaurant. A mother, father, and son came in to eat. They seemed like such a happy family. Every time I came to the table they were giggling about something. I finally figured out what all the laughter was about when they were about to leave. They got up from the table and the mom points to her son and tells me, "He has something he needs to say to you." And then the parents walk out of the restaurant leaving their son to talk to me alone.

At the time, I was newly broken hearted as my boyfriend had just broken up with me. I was not emotionally ready to start a new relationship. I needed a minute. So when he asked for my number, I told him no. But I never forgot about how kind and friendly he and his family was. And with each future subsequent failed relationship, I would reignite the thought, "If only I had said yes. If only I had been ready." A decade went by and I was still saying the same thing to myself. Five more years after that decade went by, the same thought. The recurring thought was agonizing because that regret served as a very painful reminder that I can't go back and change the past. And what was so damaging about this particular regret was that I believed it also affected my future. I thought I missed my one chance and I would never get one like it again.

As much as I could, I contradicted that mental doom with the belief that although that was a missed opportunity, another one will present itself............ eventually. Well, I would believe it sometimes and then when having a less than optimistic moment, I would re-entertain the "all is lost" theory. And when regret from the past wasn't enough misery for me, I included future regret to go along with it; I imagined how perfect my life would have been had I not blown it.

Misery and regret seem to be a package deal. If it's true that misery loves company, regret takes pictures of the company and keeps showing you the photo album.

Misery intensifies your regret. And the worst thing about regret is that it creates a pathway to hopelessness. And the worst thing about hopelessness is that it has the ability to time travel. At first, you remind yourself of your past regrets, only to mentally time travel into the future and envision the dream never comes to life, all the while effectively numbing your present happiness and satisfaction. Ain't that a b!+c#!

I believe in order to be free from the misery, we've got to identify the regrets and recognize them for the life stealing mothersugars that they are. Just in case you are not in the habit of calling out your regrets by name, here are a few of these life-limiting beliefs that need to be kicked to the curb:

It's all over because I missed that one opportunity.

There was only one person for me and now that it will never be, I am doomed for life.

I am being punished for making a mistake.

If only I had said this.

If only I had done that.

Dear Single People, please kill the "if only's" of your life. Please please stop worshipping a thought that only serves your misery. I think it is superhero brave to have faith in your dreams for the future when nothing around you supports your hopes. In my decade and a half regret vs. hope melange, God would remind me that I had faith superpowers; but the more I focused on my regret, the less I could see what good could be in store for me.

In the throes of my regret, I was, at best, able to dull its sting. But I never quite achieved freedom from it. Here's to hoping that you can and will! If and when you do, please let me know about it.

Phoenix

Mary McLaughlin

Do you still love him?
Asks my old friend and confidante
Do you still love him, your alcohol ravaged husband of nearly 40
years?

I pause, rooted in my kitchen with
Smelly splotches of wee-hours boxed red wine.
Sequestered from wildfire-smoky air I can't escape,
Greasy orange sky heavy on the dusty desiccated foliage

Of our once fragrant garden
Shriveled leaves expose bone dry dirt
tucked in by mulch, now like congealed breakfast cereal
Even the hummingbirds seem breathless, hovering

Repair the rotted windows with the expired warranty,
Or leave all, as-is, flee for worldly adventures.
Shed hopes and Grandma's paintings on my walls
Time's collections of books, vinyl, family photos
My darling dogs

Pinching at illusions
What is real? Do I love him?
... do I love me?
I am not my things.
The heart-world still beats, waiting

I remember spring's bursting promise
Crisp snowfalls, blue skies overhead,
Puppies and pregnancy
Campfires and compost

Without the wine stench and sinking anger
Hopelessness seeping
Spinning me in its heavy web
Do I fall or do I fly?

Lost and Found

Susan Johnson

When I was in second grade, Howard Branton came to school without his shirt on. It was as if no one in his family had noticed. I don't remember where the teacher found another one for him; in the "lost and found" I think.

We were unmercifully mean to him. Unmercifully mean for adults, but probably normally mean for 7 year olds. We snickered and pointed, moved chairs away from him and wouldn't play with him at recess. I don't think it was so much just the fact of his missing a shirt, but that earlier in the year he had also peed in his pants at his desk and left a milk carton so long under his papers that it grew maggots.

No one wanted to sit near Howard. I remember the way the pee ran down the floor in a little stream under his feet back behind him under Eileen and Karen before getting to me and then Dana in the back row. It was a lot of pee. Not much was said. The paper towels didn't do very much. We all went out to recess early, I think. It was like with the maggots; not much was said, they were just thrown away and something sprayed all around inside Howard's desk.

Howard was on my bus route that year and I remember his house. It was three colors; the top was bright pink, then a large square of it was green, and then there was yellow around the bottom on one side. It looked a lot like Howard had colored it with his fat broken school crayons. It had a lot of that black insulation paper hanging off of it and there were always clothes out drying on the clothesline, even in winter. I never went there to play. I can't imagine anyone ever did. It was so different. Even then, poor was different; held apart, noticed, pointed at, snickered about, excluded and not understood.

I think Howard had a younger sister, and I remember his mother in a blue apron over her dress coming to our class one day. I thought it odd even then that she came to school in an apron and didn't notice Howard coming that day without his shirt on.

But then, I knew how easy it was for parents, (mothers especially), not to notice things. Like the summer when we were up in Canada in the Thousand Islands. It was hot after a picnic lunch and everyone was reading or sleeping and no one wanted to play with me. I was eight and my mother was fond of saying, "You have to learn to entertain yourself." She bargained with me that I could walk up a small hill to a certain tree and then turn around. So I did. But they were all still reading or sleeping so I turned around again to walk a little farther.

The next six hours were spent in what I now know as the stages of grief. Although I knew from Nature Camp to sit down and wait as soon as I realized I was lost, knowing and doing at eight years old were in separate hemispheres. I now wish they had told us how hard it would be to sit, how desperately one would want to run and run against the building reality of what "lost" meant, how excruciatingly hard it would be to seemingly do nothing when in the full boil of panic.

It was like that picture in the Red Cross Lifeguard book that showed the swimmer suddenly struck with a leg cramp, all scrunched up in a tight ball with great streams of bubbles flowing from the mouth twisted in agony while the swimmer was instructed to slowly knead the muscle and not to panic. How that grimaced face hidden behind bubbles reminds me now of that stomach wrenching realization of being lost.

Because I "knew" that we were on an island, I thought I would just keep walking across and then come back around the shore to find everyone later on. We were actually on the mainland, and I ran due north for six hours as a thunderstorm approached. I remember being so annoyed that all the animals, (most notably a large porcupine), knew exactly where they were going. Scream as I did at them to "Help Me," they did not share information as they would have in a Walt Disney film. Instead they rushed off on mysterious trails in the underbrush under the darkening sky. I thought of climbing a tree to look for the water, but if I fell, I was sure I would die. Then I thought I might die anyway and that thought made me run even faster screaming louder and longer, "MOMMIE HELP ME!" It looks like a Ouija Board message now, but then it was pure, dry-mouthed, rust-tasting fear.

I bargained with God to please save me and I'd never do another bad thing ever. I ran up hills and down into swamps and when it got darker and darker and the thunder started, I picked out a large Christmas tree-like tree, and gathered branches and pine boughs to make a bed under it for the night. I had never before felt so absolutely, existentially alone.

It was then as I sat on the boughs and the big raindrops plopped on my torn sneakers that I saw the big blue football number 49 coming through the woods and heard my name being called: "SUSIE!" It was Doug, the boat boy, from our lodge. I'd had a crush on him all summer and this was just too grade B a movie moment to be true. As he yelled, "FOUND," it was called out again and again and relayed back to rings of searchers stretching through the forest. I could hear them echoing that word, "FOUND" and my name, SUSIE, again and again and again like a chorus of invisible wood nymphs I had somehow missed in my race through the trees.

The searchers had come from the lodge. When I first went missing, my father had raced back across the lake to the lodge, 20 minutes away, to ask for help. Now I wonder what that long and lonely boat ride was like for him. Then, all I thought of was Doug. Doug wanted to carry me back but that romance novel ending was too much for my New England independent and indignant spirit, even though it was now somewhat dulled by the past humbling six hours.

As a parent of a six year old when writing this, I marvel at the lack of scars I have from that ordeal. My parents must have handled it well for the only long-lasting reflex is that I always look back when I walk in the woods, just so I will have a sense of what it looks like when I turn around. I still bargain with God, but never as seriously as that day.

I had a secret feeling for years after that summer that my brother would have been happier if I'd never been found, if I had just wandered off out of his way, stopped being that small annoyance in his life. He was so powerful that the sense of him often took over our whole home like a huge black cloud nearly covering my sky. I was so convinced that my mother loved him more than me that one summer night when I was particularly annoyed, angry, hurt, and adolescent, I decided I would really "show them all." After slamming every door on the way, I struck out into a warm June night and climbed up (not very far) into a huge pine tree that sat on a hill overlooking our house and backyard.

There I sat for three hours as the lights went on in various rooms of the house (like in *Tiny Alice* I would think years later) as my mother came out on the back porch and called "S U S I E." I watched as my father conferred with my mother and went to bed, as my brother and mother watched TV, as my mother walked the dog, calling again for me, and as life went on without me. It was the inside out version of being lost in the woods. Like being on the wrong side of the x-ray. Negative and not positive. I felt like what I thought the Holy Ghost must feel like, invisible but ever present, annoyingly close but just beyond reach, watching from on high, feeling lonely and saying "Tsk, Tsk," a lot.

After two hours I was sad, still angry, now for new reasons, and cold. But I didn't know how to get out of the tree. Not in a climbing sense, but in terms of my pride. I didn't know how to get back into that house, into my life, how to save face, how to find my way back.

I did somehow just go in the back door and "harrumph" down the hall, past my mother smoking with "Johnny Carson," go into my room and close the door.

I had just seen my family without me. It was as if I had died in those woods years before and had descended like some spirit of summer past into that tree to catch up on how they were all doing without me. I found out they were all doing just fine.

In a new and more profound way that night, sobbing into my pillow, I felt as if I had just been forgotten, lost in another way. Maybe only Howard Branton would have understood.

Out of Art, Love

Mary Langer Thompson

"That's no way to treat your mother!" she said loudly as she slammed the front door.

Our grown son's girlfriend had been killed in a car accident and both my husband and I were on the phone, attempting to console him. My mother-in-law, MaryAlice, dropped in to show us a small picture-hanger hook she had found. My husband explained this was a bad time.

She stormed out, causing a crack in the wall next to the door.

Dave had recently moved both our widowed mothers, in their eighties, to the Sun City community next to our new home where we had moved so I could take a new job. His mother's new home looked like an "English cottage."

Then, because the course of any seemingly true family harmony never did run smooth for long, her granddaughter Coty became pregnant, had a fight with the father, and needed somewhere to go. MaryAlice had raised this now forty-year old who never thought she could get pregnant. Coty's mother felt she had kidnapped her and that she would someday take her back.

But time and mothers are sometimes thieves, and the years passed. None of the three women could be together long without fighting. And so it went, and so Coty came to live with MaryAlice, against our best advice, our reminders of advancing age, and our warnings concerning Coty's credit. Her response? We could just get off her deed and she would get a reverse mortgage. "Good idea," we said, but warned that the rules read that Coty and her son could only live in Sun City for a certain number of days.

Soon, the call came from Coty to my husband: "How could you have bought my grandmother this noisy washing machine and dryer?"

"It came with the house. We love ours," said my husband.

"The drapes are hideous. Why didn't you get her into a three bedroom?"

Scathing letters came next from MaryAlice. Perhaps she should never have birthed my now-in-his-sixties husband. She thought I would fall in love with Spencer once I saw his cute little face, because don't all women love all children?

She broke off her friendship with my mother.

Soon we heard rumors of her son running off with her money.

Dave stopped coming to church with my mother and me.

Why did I ever agree that my husband's mother come live near us? Because my own mother was here? Because I saw how much he loved her, despite her sending him as a teen to relatives who didn't want him for a time when his dad divorced her?

Over the next couple of years, MaryAlice stopped coming to church and took the reverse mortgage money and bought another house three blocks away and out of Sun City. Coty became her legal caretaker. All we could do was drop off birthday and Christmas cards on the front porch since they had no mailbox and ask questions of people who bumped into them. We called social workers and police to check occasionally, but nothing seemed amiss, even though they thought MaryAlice was falling too often.

It was early January when we learned from a cousin that MaryAlice had passed the previous August.

When I mentioned to a lady from church that Dave's mother had passed, she cried. She befriended MaryAlice and took her to the bank once to get her own account. Soon police were at her door telling her to stay away. She was scared.

"Oh, we should get flowers," she said, "for Sunday's service."

"I'll take care of that and I'll add your name and the church women group's name," I said.

The following Sunday when the pink flowers, MaryAlice's favorite color, sat in the front, I couldn't find any announcement in the bulletin.

"I swear," I said to my mother. "She's bullying me from the grave."

The church lady called me again. The women's group was meeting the following day, so could I bring the flowers again and say a few words? I reluctantly agreed.

Dave made a poster print of one of his mother's paintings.

How did MaryAlice maneuver that I write and deliver her one and only eulogy?

It was Valentine's Day, and the minister finished talking to the women about marital love.

I stepped up to the podium:

"MaryAlice was my mother-in-law for forty-six years, and recently passed away at age 93. She worked at Lockheed during WWII, like Rosie the Riveter. Later, as a divorced single mom, she worked as a nurse's aide until she met and married her second husband. They moved to Mt. Shasta, California from the San Fernando Valley where they raised her granddaughter, Coty.

She was an incredible artist. As a young woman she won that art contest on the back of the matchbook and a full course, which she completed. When she moved to Mt. Shasta, she enrolled in another class and the teacher took one look at her work and said, 'Go home. I have nothing to teach you.'

When I married Dave, she asked me what she could paint as a wedding present. I told her I liked street scenes. She found a black and white sepia print and spent a year painting in color what everyone thought was her best work."

At this point I walked over with the microphone to the art print, set on an easel.

I told about how my son, one Thanksgiving, mid-bite, pointed to the painting and said, "That's Grandma." I had laughed.

But now, as though looking at the painting for the first time, I studied her face and saw it really was my mother-in-law in that street that looked like it could have been in Spain or Tuscany.

Her face was lovely. She was flirting with a man that looked like my husband's father, Lee, one of the most handsome men I'd ever known, so handsome that he went on to give me two more mothers-in-law to the unbelievable heartbreak of MaryAlice. I suddenly realized she had loved him all her life. Hers wasn't a common love that you get over after a divorce. She had sent her children away to uncaring relatives in order to go into a mental hospital to recover. But she had never recovered. She pushed Dave away knowing she had raised him right and he had found his love, me. And she had raised him and his sister, so emotionally bereft that MaryAlice felt she had to raise Coty. And now Coty had a fatherless child. She martyred herself for another baby, probably hoping he'd somehow turn out to be as wonderful a man as my Dave.

Maybe her love was simply too much to bear, and she didn't know how to overcome it and heal.

And thinking of her this way, perhaps I could begin to love her.

The crack in the wall stays. It's a reminder of my own flawed heart.

FINDING TRUTH AT THE THRESHOLD OF MORTALITY

Aimee Ross

"I have a question for you, Aim," Mom says from her cornflower blue La-Z-Boy, a TV tray with toilet paper and a potty chair to her right, a table lamp with *People* magazines and her iPhone on the left.

"Okay, ready," I say while gathering Christmas ornaments and decorations the kids and I put up for her and Dad at Thanksgiving.

"How did you stay so positive during everything you went through?" she asks.

This takes me by surprise.

"Uhhhh, Prozac?" I joke, and she laughs.

She needs to laugh. I know she is scared, depressed even, awaiting her next chemo treatment.

Twenty years ago, she battled uterine cancer, but she'd stayed cancer-free ever since, a miracle.

Three months ago, she was diagnosed with cancer again: non-Hodgkin's lymphoma.

"I'm serious," Mom says, and my brain begins its search for an answer.

The Trifecta of Shit. That's what she was referring to:

· The end of my eighteen-year marriage.

· A heart attack at age forty-one, induced by stress and high blood pressure and related to anxiety.

· A near-fatal car crash, five months (to the day) later, caused by an under-the-influence young man who ran a stop sign and smashed into me and my car. He died. I barely survived.

But here I am, in this moment, alive to tell the tale. I didn't give up—maybe that's what Mom was referring to—though I wouldn't call that staying "positive." Probably because I was the one living it, not observing, like she had.

Now the roles are almost reversed.

"You know, it's funny, Mom. I had someone ask me one time how it felt fighting for my life, and I just didn't have a good answer. Same as now."

What a cop-out , I think. She needs hope. She needs inspiration. She needs a pep talk. It's the least I can do for her.

"At the time," I go on, "I didn't know I was fighting for my life, because it didn't seem like a choice. I was just doing what everyone told me to do. I don't remember being positive, Mom. I can't lie."

No real mystery, I guess, just living. And strength, I think, even though sometimes its source isn't always clear.

"Maybe it's having enough determination to see—to hope— beyond the moment?"

Mom sighs.

"Yeah, I suppose you're right," she says. "I'm trying, Aimee. I really am."

And I know that she is.

"It's just"—her voice breaks as she continues—"hard."

She lowers her head into her hands and cries through fingertips framing her face.

"I don't want to die."

But I know that she is.

"I know," I say to her quietly. "No one does."

STARK REALITY

Seven years ago, I faced my own mortality.

Not once, but twice.

Both times, Mom was by my side. I was on the phone with her when I first noticed my heart attack symptoms, and when I woke up in Intensive Care after the accident, she was standing right beside my bed. In the months after, she served as my live-in nurse, keeping me comfortable and caring for me while transporting me to my many follow-up appointments. Mom helped me in my fight so I could grow in strength.

Several existential epiphanies later, I understood that not only had I almost died, but someday, I actually would . Death was no longer an abstract noun to fear; it was real, and it was inevitable.

I thought I'd come to terms with dying. Maybe I was even okay with it.

But watching my mom die, her body taken over by a disease that could not be controlled, and witnessing Dad, her husband of forty-eight years, do everything in his power to stop it as my brother and sister and I tried to ease their burdens, made me think of my new husband and my children surrounding me in my final days, death looming. Or worse, made me imagine a life in which they were no longer present, leaving me with a terrifying, palpable emptiness.

How does a person live in a world without his spouse or her mother or his child? And how can a spirit so full of life and love and energy just disappear?

I don't understand. And I am definitely not okay with it.

TRANSCENDENTAL INSIGHT

I like to think that Mom helped me to live again, and then I helped her to die.

And there are truths I understand now, truths that can be uncovered only by confronting mortality—which I have—time and again.

I know that I am lucky, thankful, and content to be alive—every single day.

I know that life can be serendipitous, but also fickle, changing within a split second of two cars crashing or across a nine-month span of a disease growing.

I also know that neither the past nor the future exists, only the present moment, and it is of the utmost importance.

Because the present moment might be exactly where I am supposed to be.

And ultimately, I know that in my struggle to actualize death, I will be forever navigating a gray area between acceptance and denial.

Aren't we all?

MYSTERIOUS MOMENTS: THOUGHTS THAT TRANSFORM GRIEF (EXCERPT)

Jane Williams

Over the past 25 years, I have been a hospital clinical psychologist, working with children and families experiencing trauma, life-threatening illness, and loss. When I started my career, the literature about grief was in its infancy. Research on grief has increased, but it is difficult work requiring a lengthy investment of time to understand its essence.

Over the years, I have developed a set of beliefs about how people experience grief.

Some of these beliefs are supported by research, some are based on theory, and some rely on my clinical experiences. In this set of beliefs, there is one remarkable observation—sometimes people have transformative thoughts that dramatically change their experience of grief. These experiences form the basis for a book I have recently written.

I believe that grief is a process. In the late 1960s, Elizabeth Kubler-Ross published her first book, *On Death and Dying*,[1] based on research with dying individuals. Her writings opened the door to a previously undiscussed topic and set the stage for increased understanding of the emotional experience of dying. She outlined psychological stages, including denial, anger, bargaining, despair, and acceptance, which dying individuals may undergo.

Later, these same stages were applied to grieving individuals, with the notion that passage through the phases would result in "acceptance" of loss. The application of the stages of dying to the stages of grieving often led people to expect a prescribed cycle of grief. Grieving individuals understandably felt surprised and disappointed when they did not experience certain set stages. They felt that they had "failed" grief when acceptance didn't arrive on schedule. In my reading, research, and work with grieving individuals, I came to see grief as a dynamic, ongoing process, not an event with a set series of psychological tasks completed in a specific order. Like a meandering stream, the process of grief has a direction and timing of its own.

There are no set time limits for grief. Contrary to many of our cultural expectations, so-called "closure" does not come with the funeral. We cannot "will" grief to start or stop. We want grief to hurry up and end, and we are sometimes perplexed and distressed by its tenacity. Time seems to stand still. As CS Lewis wrote, "I not only live each endless day in grief, but live each day thinking about living each day in grief."[2]

Early in the process, time feels like an enemy, but as in many processes, time can eventually help us heal and grow.

There are common feelings and emotions that may be experienced during grief, but I believe that grief is a highly individualistic process. There is no prediction of how a particular person will respond to a particular loss. In fact, we are sometimes surprised at the strength of emotion that we may feel with a specific loss, yet we are equally surprised with an absence of strong emotion with other losses. Individuals experience loss in their life in unique ways. Some experience intense sadness initially, while sadness comes later for others. For some, sorrow may come in spurts or not at all. Some cry freely and express their distress openly. Others cry in private, hold back tears, or don't even feel moved to cry. Some need to talk constantly about their grief while others are uncomfortable talking about it. Some prefer not to talk but feel better doing tasks or returning to work. Some children cannot concentrate on school tasks, while others throw themselves into their schoolwork. The experience and expression of grief is deeply personal and highly idiosyncratic.

Because of the personal and varying nature of grief, I believe that narratives—stories—are critically important and helpful both for accepting death and coping with loss. Initially, we often need to tell our story of a death over and over to ourselves internally or to others. This helps us assimilate what has happened. It is almost as if we need to imprint the experience to make it real.

I once had a wise mentor who was supervising my work with a patient who kept telling his history over and over. I asked her when she thought he would stop repeating the story. "When he no longer needs to," she said. We are all like this patient: we tell our stories of loss until we no longer "need to."

With the passage of time, the initial narrative often changes, and details are added or taken away. Often the memory of other personal characteristics and relational experiences allow for a more holistic view of the person who died, including both positive and negative qualities. This incorporation of added memories allows us to experience a broader range of emotions involved in the loss. When my father died, my narrative focused on the alleviation of his suffering. He had a very difficult final six months, and I both felt and described his death as a "blessing." With time, my story began to include more memories of our earlier relationship that opened me up to my sadness at his death. My story—our stories—change over time and help us accommodate our loss.

Our stories help to make meaning out of loss. In the psychological theory known as constructivism, "meaning reconstruction" is posited as the central process in grief.[3]

By creating and telling our narratives, we try to make meaning out of our suffering.

The creation of our stories is an active, unconscious process and influenced by both old and new life experiences, such as the birth of a baby in a family following the death of an older child. Over time, our narratives often evolve into a deeper interpretation of our loss experiences. This meaning-making process can result in positive growth for each of us.

Given my belief that grief is an idiosyncratic, meaning-making process with no time limits and best reflected in narratives, I haven't been surprised when grief-stricken individuals tell me of sudden moments when they have experienced transformative thoughts. These "mysterious moments" don't result from a conscious intent; their source is unclear. During these moments, the griever experiences thoughts that reframe his or her grief. They are like the "aha!" moments when, suddenly, we somehow see the world differently. The unexplainable thoughts tend to come "out of nowhere," whether the griever is focused on loss or not. The thoughts may occur when our loved one is dying, in the early period following the death, or after many years have passed. They are unique to each individual, weaving together the past and present within the psyche. I find that their occurrence is not universal; they are more often associated with deaths that have caused the bereaved ongoing distress.

These thoughts are often breakthroughs that offer relief and healing. My book, *Mysterious Moments: Thoughts That Transform Grief,* is written about these meaningful moments, these epiphanies, when individuals suddenly see or understand their loss in a new way.

Reading about the experiences of others can decrease the feeling of isolation, encourage the sense of survival, and provide a spark to lighten another's path through the dark process of grief.

REFERENCES

1. Kubler-Ross, E. (1969). On death and dying. New York: Scribner.

2. Lewis, C. S. (1961). A grief observed. United Kingdom: Faber and Faber.

3. Neimeyer, R. A. (1998). Lessons of loss: A guide to coping. New York: McGraw-Hill.

4. Bearison, D. J. (2006). When treatment fails: How medicine cares for dying children. New York: Oxford University Press.

DURING

My Loved One Has Died, Here's How You Can Help

Elizabeth Coplan

Few people I know are as organized as my friend Kate Ruffing. Kate recorded several podcasts for Grief Dialogues, sharing her experience as a young widow. Kate found it hard to focus while her husband lay dying in his hospital bed. There were to-do's to be done at home. The dogs needed walking. The grass was growing in the sidewalk cracks. The front porch light fixture needed its light bulb changed. It didn't look like anyone was home. They weren't.

So Kate began to make lists, lists of household tasks. Before long, her lists were long and her husband's time short. She needed help and discovered that while many will want to help when they hear of your loss, they honestly don't know what to do.

They'll say "Call me if you need me." They mean well, and may even do something wonderful out of kindness, but it's not what you need.

Here are a few ideas for you to share with your family and friends when you are in need. Add other ideas. Delete those that don't apply. Be as specific as you can, if you can. Post the list on your front door.

I appreciate that you are here.
Thank you for asking how you can help.
Here's a list of what I need done:
• Write me a card of encouragement (but please don't say my loss "is for the best"}
• Leave a basket of fruit on my doorstep (ring the bell, then run away)
• Give me a hug
• Share a memory of my loved one (in person or in a card)
• Send an email or text every once in a while to let me know you are thinking of me or simply let me know you care
• Tell me what I mean to you or why I matter
• Do something special for someone I take care of (e.g. my son or daughter)
• Pull the weeds in my garden
• Mow my yard

- Wash my car
- Walk my dogs
- Invite me to do something fun
- Donate to a cause you know I support
- Send me a text or give me a call when you are going to the store and ask if I need anything
- Prepare my dinner (something that can be frozen if I don't need it that night)
- Clean something in my house (if you know me well you will know what that something might be)
- Hire a housekeeper for me
- Schedule a spa treatment for me, pay for it, and offer to drive me there

As the person struggling through grief, you must NOT be strong or brave and you may or you may not "get over it" anytime soon. However, your true friends will want to help in some way. They mean well. They need to be instructed.

Don't think too hard on your list. "Do my dishes" is a perfectly acceptable requested task. Just a couple of items on your list is all you need. It's a start.

Under the Crabapple Trees

Alison Eckels

The hurricane had blasted through just four days earlier, and many houses were still without electricity. A cousin's house just up the hill had lights, so my parents walked up there to read that evening.

As they were getting ready to return home, Dad looked pale. Mom offered to get the car but he insisted on walking ....across the street and down the hill and in at the once-upon-a-time scallop shell driveway, past the shed and almost to the crabapple trees.

He fell there.

He had fallen a number of times before. With help my mother had been able to get him up each time. But neighbors' houses were dark and she didn't want to bother anyone who might be sleeping.

So she called the police. Two young policemen arrived and addressed my father kindly with the words, "Can we help you, sir?"

"Oh no, I'm all right," he replied in his characteristic fashion.

They leaned down to take his hands and he reached up to them. As they brought him to his feet, he slumped, and my mother knew in that instant he was gone.

He was. But a 9-1-1 call dictates what will follow.

The young men began CPR as my mother wrung her hands and said over and over,

"Stop! He has a living will! He's 91 years old! He's ready to die! Leave him alone!!"

To no avail.

She hated what they were doing to his body.

Afterwards she grieved mightily that she had not stayed beside him, holding his hand, kissing him, saying good-bye.

Instead she went inside, the flashlight from her walk lighting her way. She tried to call her doctor to somehow avert this awful mess. It was past 9:00 and the best she could do was leave a message.

An ambulance came. I presume that they continued CPR all the way to the hospital.

Was it his doctor who came and pronounced him dead?

She didn't call any of us that night.

I just know that when the phone rang the next morning and my husband answered it and said her name aloud, we both knew exactly why she was calling.

My father had been quite senile for ten years before he died. Friendly, charming, he introduced himself four times to the same person in the course of a party. I lived far away with my husband and young children during those years--- having no real idea of the Life-Job my mother was doing.

For all the rest of my life Dad had been a busy hard-working doctor, doing house calls even at night right up until age 81 when my family took away the car keys.

My loss was not a close gut-wrenching one; but more a huge gaping hole where someone had always been, never very present, but there.

All that explanation aside, when Dad died, I got a glimpse of spirit.

By the crabapple tree - I could see him as a bright orb of light shining above his body on the grass.

Where my mother grieved at what she had let happen, I saw him marveling, filled with curiosity:

"What are they doing? What are they doing now??"

At what point did he recognize that that was his body the young policemen were working on? At what point did he make the more astonishing discovery that he was spirit, a spark of light, leaving his earthly shell behind?

Ten or fifteen years earlier my sister had asked Dad if he believed in God. "No," was his direct answer. "Why do you go to church then?" she persisted. "Habit," he replied.

Dad said he didn't need any help from the policemen, and yet he raised up his arms.

Who was he looking at? What did he see?

I believe that he saw something else when the young policemen reached down their hands to him: he saw and reached up to the two angels who were there to help him cross over.

"Oh, no, I'm all right." It was what he truly believed about himself. And it was true in that moment. He was all right. He was ready to go. And my mother knew it.

I pondered these things, reflecting on that orb of light, astounded that what I believe but cannot possibly intellectualize could be there for me to see. And when I went again to look at his body in my mind's eye, picturing it there beneath the crabapple trees, I discovered that all he had left behind.....was his overcoat.

The overcoat that went with his hat and his doctor's bag.

The overcoat that dressed the man who gave rough, scratchy abrupt kisses, who never seemed to have a clue about what was happening in my life.

The overcoat that he wore on those countless house calls and hospital visits, recognizable to all his patients who adored him because he listened to them and heard about their aches and woes.

The overcoat that dressed the man who had grown up in a world with rules and values and judgments which he easily, freely, glibly applied.

I had received those judgments so often, and had fought and resisted them so hard.

Now, he had left his overcoat on the grass.

And I could see that the bright light which was him was not carrying the coat or the bag or the judgments with him on this next journey.

The judgments were in the overcoat pockets. He had no more need of them.

And here I was still carrying them – all the judgments I had taken on!

He was unburdened.

And he was showing me that we are spirit and we are all indeed all right.

WHEN YOUR DAD IS DYING

Maureen Geraghty

You might find yourself at a computer at 2:30 a.m.
writing thoughts about things like carefully sorting
14 bottles of pills into a.m./p.m. plastic Sunday, Monday, Tuesday...box
but you don't know what day is today-
time has morphed into doctor appointments, moments waiting, wait-
ing, sitting waiting
for a nurse, a prescription, for the right time to bring it up.
Tender moments when he tells you what he's proud of: three decent
children, going to college, being the quarterback in a single college
game, sober for nearly 3 decades.

At the kitchen table, after a second nap
he tells stories-the time his father found work during The Depression
celebrating
with a family trip to A&W for root beer and a burger. The way he still
remembers
the frosted mug, cold nickel in hand.
How he used to run and run in football practice yet now
taking a shower seems superhuman physical feat.

And while you're writing this, you consider others may find it morbid
or sad or disrespectful to document this intimate time but your next
thought
tells you it is anything but... because what you are witnessing is your
father's
aliveness. You step into time that s l o w s into moments, gestures,
wonderous routine.
In between medicines with too many vowels, hum of oxygen tank,
Band-Aids scattered on skin that takes near nothing
to bring it to pools of baby aspirined-blood,
In between dozens of hand written notes-
spin numbers, phone numbers, grocery list scrawl,
half eaten toast on a paper plate, piles of newspaper, chachka catalogs-
We are daughter and father, sharing a day.

And even after the 37th health care worker asks how he is, Dad still responds,
"Tall, dark and handsome" though he is seated in a wheelchair,
puffy steroid cheeks, squeaky hearing aid song.

When your dad is dying
you wonder how on earth you will get on that plane to go home,
how you will leave him
even though you're so burned out now from the tedium, vigilance, hygienic tasks.
You also know how damn lucky you are to absorb his being.
All day you couldn't cry because of required business, because you needed to be strong, because you knew you wouldn't stop & it's not about you now.
But at 2:30 in the morning, while oxygen tube snakes on shag carpet, you find tears tumbling, fogging up your cheaters.
Some of this crying is the stuff of loss.
How you can't imagine a world that doesn't hold him.
You also realize, you also remember, that he's still alive. A voice deep down reminds, "Be with him in all the moments now." So you decide to put the computer away, get some sleep
then a memory slips in of the other night
when your father made it to his bed, labored breathing.
You put the covers over him.
He looked up smiling a denture-less grin, stared at you with moist eyes and whispered,
"Oh, I feel so cozy."

Early Departure
A Prayer and Poem in
Three Voices

Sarah J Glerum

I was in the car, crying about my mid-life friend as I drove. Although indignant, deep down I knew this to be a random event. Shit happens, as the saying goes. Then suddenly I knew what to pray for.

Prayer

*Please let her know
the pleasure of the whole meal,
so if she has to leave the table early,
at least she will feel completely full.
Amen*

Lovely Meal

Before you push away from the table where
we've been chewing and chatting for a couple hours
(or was it days and years, maybe a half-century?)
I need to know something.
Did you get what you need to feel nourished?

Did you enjoy the succulent tidbits,
the fragrant sauces?
Do you feel satisfied?
Satiated?
Finished?
What I want most
is to hear 'yes' to this: "Are you full?"
You helped yourself to generous portions,
while regaling us with stories from your life.

You raved over the fragrance of sauces and
flowers, inhaling other people's passions,
probing for opinions on topical concerns.
You raised your voice in disagreement sometimes,
furious to make another see your point.

And, of course, not everything was edible, what with
the inevitable gristle, bone, husks or pits.
But the yummy stuff . . . laughter, candlelight,
intimacy? Did you get enough?
I want to imagine your taste buds sated with
sweet, savory, salty, along with the bitter.

Please don't say you went away hungry.
The servings were intended to be plentiful.
I know you reached for an array of concoctions
and spooned them onto your plate with gusto.
Cut, snip, mash, dip . . .I saw food disappear,

but I need to be sure you're really done.
Won't you help yourself to another dessert and coffee—
several cups—before you push yourself away
from the table and depart?
If you have to leave early,
I want you to feel stuffed with hope and
laden with contentment. Ready for your destination.

How Dare She

How *dare* she
leave early! She might as well
slam her chair against the table's edge
and stomp off. At my table, people ask
to be excused, plea for the courtesy
of a forgiving smile before heading for
in a rush to their next destination.

How *dare* she
disappear while the rest of us still eat,
with her plate half full, her wine
half-drunk—her glass smeared with

lipstick and fingerprints, residue
of what we thought would be enjoyable.

How *dare* she
create this breech of etiquette,
such an inconsiderate rupture in
the rhythm of pleasure for the rest of us.
No murmur of thanks or folding her napkin—
the subsequent destination sovereign.

How *dare* she ruin it for those
of us who want to hang back and
relax awhile before we leave.

Disappearing Act

You can't just slink away like
a misunderstood teen. Please
linger over dessert! Maybe
sip dark espresso from a
dainty cup in the silken
twilight. Please stay.
Our meal has been
sweeter because
of you. Let me
put the water
on for tea?
Please
don't
go!

A WOLF

Tess Williams

August is a time of harvest fairs, bluegrass music and fresh apple cider.

It's when I can peaches and see them glisten in their shiny glass jars on the pantry shelf.

It's when dahlias burst forth, red racing with plum to see who produces the most blossoms and it's also when my body, feeling abundance, becomes pregnant. If I was a rabbit, all it would take is 33 days to gestate and if I was a wolf, 61, but I'm a human and I needed to stay pregnant for close to 266 days. I have never made it past a wolf.

My kids and I pulled into the driveway. We had groceries and two pumpkins, since Halloween was the next day.

"Can you help me carry stuff?" I asked, because I'm not feeling well I thought. Dark haired graceful Ariana, my Persian daughter, carried a light bag, and chunky blond Sasha, my Russian son, carried his pumpkin. They helped me make a few trips, and our counter was soon stacked with cereal, organic popcorn, and walnuts.

"Can we make pumpkin seeds?" asked my daughter?

"Of course," I said smiling. "Let's put some newspaper on the floor."

I cut the tops off of the pumpkins feeling the familiar, dreaded cramping.

"Here's a spoon for you Ariana, and one for you, Sasha. Put your seeds and goo in the bowl sitting next to your pumpkin. I'll be right back".

I hurried to the bathroom biting my hand to keep from crying out. Out in a gush of blood, the baby I'd hoped for arrived, looking like a translucent plum.

I had no choice but to wash my face and help my children carve jack-o-lantern faces. But first, while they were busy scraping out their pumpkins, I snuck out the door to bury my plum beneath our white camellia tree.

"Do you want a friendly or mad looking pumpkin? "I asked each child walking towards them while tying on an apron.

Wolves always take care of their young.

I Weep for You, for Us, Momma

Jennifer Coates

It is our collective complacency that killed this calf.
His mother holds him and his little open mouth aloft
for all to see and it breaks
our hearts.
She won't let him drop to the sea floor where we could pretend his
birth into stillness didn't happen.
We don't want
to look.

It hurts too much to carry
the impossible weight of our own
responsibility for her grief,
the grief she
and her family share with us in a plea
to look
and acknowledge.
And yet we must, we must, we must
see what we've done and are doing,
over and over, everywhere
to the miraculous beauty into which we ourselves
have been born.
This mother's raw expression
washes over the mundane action and inaction we
distract ourselves with,
dissolving me into weeping that doesn't stop,
a weeping made of the same salty
undulation she
swims in.

A tidal wave of keening moves through my body
every time I think of the orca mother,
which is all the time,
a wailing
I allow to erupt in full as I drive

around my life
in the car, containing it to
a quieter, yet no less complete shuddering
in my office and behind
closed doors
in my home. I am struck by an urgent,
all-encompassing
sense of loss
that consumes me now, like never before,
—even when my own mother
died.

J-35 is the Mother I need to speak to, to embrace. I call out to her
—Momma, Momma, Momma, please
hear my prayer of love to you
in your letting go of what
we mothers can never let go of, the love of our children. I tell her
that I care
more deeply than I
can bear in this fragile body that feels her child's death as a throbbing
in my own womb.
I touch her with my mind,
through the tears
burying everything else
I ever thought was important, to say
I am
so very
sorry.

LOSING OUR TWO CHILDREN

Richard Rosario

My parents rented a small lakeside bungalow in the town where my mother grew up. My wife, Wendy, the kids, and I visited every nearly every Sunday. This particular Sunday was a warm fall day. The kids played by the lake with my mom after lunch. Then, they snacked on summer sausage and frosted circus animal cookies. As usual, there was always some to take home.

I was attending bible college. I managed to schedule my classes for four days a week. I had Monday mornings free. The apartment was government subsidized for families with children and seniors. There were three retention ponds on the property which was surrounded by oaks and other trees. The pond nearest our apartment was fifty feet from our front door.

I didn't have to be at the publishing company until the afternoon. Wendy got home from work at seven a.m. and went straight to bed. The kids insisted on having sausage and animal cookies for breakfast. I relented.

I had a paper due for my "Life of Christ" class. It was written, but I needed to type it. I didn't have a typewriter, so I left early for work, locking the door. The last thing I told the children was, "Do not touch the front door." Wendy was still sleeping. I didn't have the heart to wake her, so I left her door open, so she could hear the children. However, being exhausted, Wendy fell into a deep, deep sleep.

At about two p.m., one of the office workers called out to me, "Your wife is on the phone and she's crying."

I rushed to the phone. Wendy managed to eke out, "There's been an accident." It was all I heard.

"I'm on my way." I responded.

I had tunnel vision as I sped the car toward home.

When I reached the T-intersection to turn up the street to our apartment I saw the pastor's car approaching. I stopped my car in the middle of the street. I got out. The pastor stopped his car and got out.

"Did you hear..." was all I could say. The pastor nodded.

"I was on my way there." He replied. We both filled in the blanks of each other's incomplete sentences. We both got in our cars. I turned up the road and he followed.

"God, please don't let them die." I prayed out loud. I imagined the kids got out of house and got hit by a car in the parking lot. I never thought about the pond fifty feet from our front door.

I drove up the long drive between two of the ponds and saw two ambulances, a fire truck, and a police car. I parked my car near one of the ambulances and ran for my front door. The pastor was less than a minute behind me. I was greeted at the open front door to my apartment by a woman in a business suit.

"I'm the county coroner. Your two children have been pronounced dead." She said very professionally. It did not take any time for the words to sink in. I had already expected the worst on the short, frantic two-mile drive home. My eyes scanned the living room. It was quite crowded, but I could only see people individually. My eyes searched for Wendy. There were two neighbor women milling about the room. One was picking up toys. Wendy was seated on the couch. She was hunched over. Her face was red, and she was weeping profusely. I was numb.

Reflexively, I proclaimed my faith in God for everyone in the room to hear.

"I don't know why this has happened, but I will serve God anyway." I proclaimed for everyone to hear. The room was a swirl of activity. The woman picking up toys wanted to take them away, so they would not upset us. Wendy and I told her to leave them where they were. We were not ready to part with any of the kids' belongings.

A child services investigator and a police detective questioned us. The police detective was a member of our church. The pastor had seen to it he was called to come to shield us from further trauma. Both officials did their duties to question us. We numbly answered the questions with little emotion.

I knew I was to blame. Officially, the investigators fixed the blame on Wendy, because she was home with the children, but I was the one who did not wake her. She was asleep when I left. There was nothing she could have done. I lived with the truth then. I never allowed myself to feel guilt. Guilt was not bringing back my children.

Meanwhile, the paramedics worked feverishly to try to revive the children even though they had been under the water for an undetermined period of time. Because it was fall, the water might just be cold enough to put the children's bodies into a suspended state keeping their brain functions from ceasing.

The paramedics were able to revive Matthew just enough to put him on life support. They continued to try to revive Sarah. Both children were taken to the nearby hospital, the same one where Sarah had been born.

Doctors and nurses worked feverishly to revive Sarah. Matthew did not regain consciousness, but was on life support. Wendy and I were ushered to a family waiting room. The pastor, his wife, and an elder of the church joined us. We all prayed as hard as we could. Wendy and I verbally encouraged Sarah from the little room.

"C'mon, Sarah. Be tough." We said.

Another nurse came to the room. She wheeled in a hysterical woman in a wheelchair. It was the young neighbor woman who was the first person to see the children in the pond. She was babbling incoherently. I asked the nurse to take her somewhere else. I couldn't deal with her hysterics and my own grief at the same time. The nurse wheeled her away.

"I'm freezing." I said. A nurse brought me a warmed blanket. We kept praying. Another nurse came to the room.

"I'm sorry." She said. "We were unable to revive your daughter. You can go see her.

There is no change in your son's condition."

We all wept. Wendy and I followed the nurse to the gurney where Sarah lay still, quiet, like she was sleeping. Our family doctor had been called. We wept. The pastor wept. Our doctor wept. He had delivered Sarah.

Wendy bent over Sarah and kissed her forehead. I moved closer.

"I'll see you soon." I said. I kissed Sarah's forehead. It was already cool.

We returned to the waiting room. A nurse told us Matthew was going to be heli-ported to Swedish American Hospital in Rockford, which specialized in pediatric near drownings.

I needed to call my parents. I reached for the phone on the wall above one of the chairs in the room. I punched in my parents' phone number. My mom answered.

"Mom, you need to sit down." I said. It was cliché, but it borne from a real concern she might collapse. "Sarah is dead. Matthew is in critical condition."

"What! How?" My mom responded. She didn't question the words themselves. My dad in typical fashion overhearing only my mom's side of the conversation, kept shouting in the background demanding to know what was going on. He finally snatched the phone from my mom.

"What's going on?" He asked frantically.

"Sarah is with Jesus. Matthew is in critical condition."

"No...We need to..." My dad attempted to reply. He instantly wanted to undo time. "How could..." He couldn't finish any question because he didn't know what to ask. I told them we were preparing to go to the hospital in Rockford. The pastor and his wife drove. A steady rain fell as Wendy and I sat in the backseat silently staring blankly at the passing farm fields.

When we arrived, we were met by my parents. We shared the elevator with a doctor treating Matthew.

"There is very little brain activity." He explained.

"Can we just end this now?" I asked. I understood there was little chance Matthew would ever be Matthew again. At best, we were looking at a permanent, vegetative state.

"No. We have to everything possible..." My dad blurted out.

The doctor explained, by law, Matthew would remain on life support, but if brain death occurred life support would be shut off.

We began our vigil. We met with hospital administrators, the chaplain, social workers, a ventilator care facility representative and a variety of other people. It all was a blur. At the same time, we were talking to the funeral home director and planning Sarah's funeral.

The hospital gave us a hotel room in the hospital. Wendy and I slept there each night. We were able to see Matthew anytime we wanted, and we had a special hotline to call the nurses for an update on his condition anytime we wanted.

Wendy and I lived in isolated bubbles. We were isolated from everyone around us. We were isolated from each other. We were alone in our grief.

I awoke each morning and cried in the shower. Then, I dressed and walked the neighborhood around the hospital. I resorted to my old fallback comfort—food. I ate, and I ate, and I ate. I denied myself nothing. I ate breakfast, lunch and dinner in the hospital cafeteria with desserts accompanying each meal.

I could not tell you what Wendy felt or experienced. I could not feel or experience anything outside of myself. In some ways, I have felt completely insular ever since. No one around us could identify with the magnitude of our losses as they constantly confirmed in a desperate attempt to comfort us and themselves.

The week passed in a fog. Family and friends descended upon us. I spent each day hosting people in the pediatric intensive care unit family waiting room. My cousins who had lost a brother to drowning came to share their condolences. The pastor of the church sat with me and talked about such banal things as how to properly make a root beer float. It was far better than praying or quoting scripture verses. He did plenty of that as well, but those things were empty to us.

There was only one thing left I could pray for—Matthew's death. If we couldn't have him back as a conscious little boy we prayed God would take him. We couldn't bear the prospect of the monetary or emotional expenses of a perpetual wake. Wendy and I prayed it would end.

The doctor told us they needed to know if Matthew should be designated DNR, "Do Not Resuscitate." We struggled with the decision. We wanted the saga to end, but we didn't want it to end, because the end meant the end of Matthew.

Wendy and I sat in the chapel. We prayed. We talked. The pastor joined us. Again, his best advice was not a bible verse or platitude, but very human.

"It doesn't matter which choice you make, nature will take its course." He said.

Wendy and I decided for the DNR. We wanted our son back, but not in a vegetative state.

We prayed Matthew's brain would shut down.

Sarah's funeral was set for Friday. We had lived in the hospital hotel room since Monday night and decided Friday would be our last day of vigil there. We would go home for the funeral and back to our now childless apartment.

I had no clothes for a funeral. Fortunately, money had been trickling in from donations.

People put a few bucks in our hands everywhere we went. They knew we were financially devastated. I went to a clothing store near the hospital. I told the salesperson I was buying clothes for my daughter's wedding to Jesus.

The church was packed for Sarah's funeral. Friends, relatives, fellow church members, classmates from the bible college, and members of the rescue squad attended.

I spent the time before the funeral running around playing host and thanking people for coming. People remarked about our faith and our strength. We were in shock. It would last an entire year, and in some ways the rest of our lives.

A local newspaper said we cried and sang. I know I did both. I raised my hands and sang praises to God. I believed Sarah could be raised from the dead if it was God's will. I didn't expect it to happen, though.

Sarah was buried by a big evergreen tree. The grave is marked only by a cemetery issued plaque. We did not have any money to buy headstones, nor did we see any reason. Sarah was gone.

Meanwhile, Matthew still lay on life support in Rockford. We had a direct hotline number to the hospital. They would call if there was any change. There was nothing more we could do.

There was very little chance Matthew would ever regain consciousness which I had known since talking to the attending doctor the first night in the elevator.

As the new week began, we relied on calling the hospital. There was no change in Matthew's condition. There was further talk about a timetable to move him to a ventilator care facility if he persisted in a vegetative state. We continued to hope the end would come naturally.

Two days later, the phone rang. It was the call. Matthew's brain was shutting down. We were told to come to the hospital to say goodbye. There Matthew lay with tubes and the breathing apparatus attached, motionless as he had been since the day he drowned. In our minds, he died the same day Sarah did. We said goodbye.

There was another funeral to plan. Many of the people who attended Sarah's funeral sent condolences and apologized they were not able to make it back for a second funeral. Some, even relatives, apologized they could not make it because they could not bear it. I thought to myself,

"You think this is hard for you?" I did not begrudge them though. It would have been hard for anyone to be around that much sorrow. Even so, the church was mostly full for Matthew's funeral. Matthew was buried right next to Sarah where he belonged.

The funerals were over, but we were still a curiosity. Everywhere we went there were the whispers. We were "those people whose kids drowned." The accident had been front page news for several days. People debated our fault and responsibility in the letters to the editor pages.

Friends wrote responses to defend us. We were aware of them. I read the newspapers. I kept them for many years before finally realizing all the get well cards sent to Matthew and all of the condolence cards and letters served no purpose. They were things I would not return to look at again, so I finally threw them away. I made a point to cling to no physical object belonging to the children because nothing would bring them back again.

We were invited to homes for dinner. People would sit politely across the table and watch us as if we were celebrities and wonder what made us tick. They wanted to ask a million questions, but were unsure any of them were appropriate.

However, it was only a matter of weeks before people became immersed in their own lives again. We were fine with that. We didn't need anyone reminding us who we were. Wendy and I were consigned to think of Matthew and Sarah, and remember them and their deaths every day for the rest of our lives. For years, my first thought upon waking would be, "Matthew and Sarah are dead."

In November, Wendy had a routine doctor visit. When I got home she told me she had some news.

"I'm pregnant." She said.

We were both shocked. This time it was a good shock. However, I wondered what I would do about school. We figured Wendy could work for at least six more months, so I could finish the school year.

The doctor scheduled an ultrasound for Wendy's second appointment. When I got home Wendy was very excited. She put the ultrasound on the table.

"Here's the first baby." She said. "And here's the second baby."

"Twins." I said. "They will be a boy and girl! I know it! It's a miracle!"

The doctor scheduled Wendy for a caesarean on August 5 th . It was the same doctor who had delivered Sarah. The pregnancy went fine. Wendy was very large and uncomfortable, but there were no complications. She wasn't even put on bed rest until the last week.

However, four days before the caesarean appointment, Wendy woke me in the early morning to tell me she was in labor. I quickly showered to wake up. Wendy told me to hurry.

We were at the hospital in minutes. The first twin was already trying to break out of her womb, except it was breach. There was no stopping the baby. The first twin backed out into the world butt first, ripping Wendy's cervix.

The second twin was now wedged sideways and was coming out one arm first. The doctor ordered an emergency C-section. Wendy was immediately anesthetized. The surgeon wasted no time. He didn't perform a pretty bikini-cut. He managed to rescue the second twin before Wendy's womb began to collapse on it. It was a boy and a girl, in that order. The boy weighed six pounds, four ounces. The girl weighed five pounds, fifteen ounces.

However, Wendy was not perfectly healthy. The doctor determined she was still bleeding heavily. She was prepped for surgery to locate and stop the bleeding. A doctor informed me she might need a hysterectomy. He was seeking my consent. I stopped him and told him, "Of course, I consent. Do whatever you have to save my wife."

The twins were ready to go home the next day, but Wendy needed a week in the hospital to recover. She finally got to see the twins after an entire day. The twins stayed with her in the hospital so she could bond with them.

People called me a modern Job. I was a 'man of God.' I had been tested. I had lost everything. God had restored me.

Everyone who heard our story declared it a miracle. Matthew and Sarah drowned on September 28, 1987. Michael and Rachael were born on August 1, 1988. Ten months and four days elapsed between the two occurrences—308 days, 296 days if you subtracted the twelve days before Matthew was declared brain dead.

Of course, my wife and I have gone through many changes. She went on to become a corrections officer. I eventually went back to university and earned a bachelor's degree with honors as a student of distinction in political science, a juris doctor, and a master's degree in education. I practiced law in Illinois for six years before becoming a public school teacher in 2005 in Las Vegas, Nevada.

My wife and I are no longer Christians. We are both atheists. The loss of our children had nothing to do with the cessation of our faith. It was borne out of a lifelong study of scriptures, sacred writings and religions from around the world. I reached the conclusion of atheism based upon reason and logic, not a disappointment with religion.

Today, Michael and Rachael are 30 years old. Their younger sister, Brittany, is 27 years old. Rachael has provided us with four grandchildren, two for whom she chose adoption.

For the Dying and the Ones with Them

Maureen Geraghty

Every day we wrack our minds
over injustice, disease, violence, loss
looking under every stone for The answer-
some shiny elixir that will take it all away, fairly
with someone, or more than one or God or no God to blame.
Maybe we are asking the wrong questions
Maybe we're not looking deeper, or wider or differently-
our gaze so stuck on the wounds.
In the rubble between ashes,
there are hands holding the dead.
Love brave enough to lie beside the excruciating
Until all sacrifice makes sense
Until word weapons and tears
cease with the last breath of a boy, so loved.
Everyone drops an opinion
Stands in the silence
of life meeting the other life,
feels the pulse of everyone beating, in unison
as the Angels shimmer with a light
we can All see
and the right answer is only
Love.

A Journey With Breast Cancer

Aspen Drake

My mom was first diagnosed with breast cancer when my siblings and I were too little to fully grasp the situation. We did know that we didn't like going to the hospital. It was bright and smelled weird, and the frail lady in the bed wasn't mom. Relatives came and went and got us to school, and eventually we were coming home to mom again. She was tired and sickly, but she gained strength and spirit those next few months.

We carried on as young families do, spending the days in school, the evenings fighting bedtime and dessert caps, and the weekends at sports tournaments. She taught special ed at a local middle school, but even after a full day of working with challenging children, she was happy to return to a house full of her own. Challenging children being a term I use of my own accord, my mother being so incredibly patient that she never spoke ill to or of a student. Life felt busy and full, and mom supported all four of us siblings with every moment and spare penny she had. Until the summer of my senior year when we discovered the cancer had returned. That was an anxious transitional time for me, having my mom be sick again and facing the prospect of being shipped off to college. Try as I might to stay home to selflessly support my family (aka totally give in to my anxieties) my mom vowed she would send me to school, if it was the last thing she did. I am so grateful that she did. I am even more grateful to say that she made it to my graduation a few years later.

It was when I returned home from college that things began to decline. The cancer became increasingly aggressive. I watched my cheerful busybody of a mother become tired and sick again. She went in weekly for chemo and testing, and spent most of the time at home in her room resting. I think often she was too uncomfortable to sleep. I have fond memories of sitting in the kitchen at 2 in the morning making food, or on my computer, and having a random visit from mom as she made her trip downstairs for the night. I could tell she was wary, but she still would joke with me and chat before making her way to her room again. That is one of the things I miss about my mom. She is the only person who would ever be genuinely interested in anything I had to say, just because I was saying it. Moms are magical like that.

I remember one morning I got up for work and mom was downstairs waiting on the couch. She told me she had a doctors appointment and was waiting to be picked up. I felt like something was off, so I checked her calendar. There was no appointment that day. I helped mom back into her bed and left for work. Later that evening I got a call that my mother had been admitted into the hospital. She was low on sodium and that had caused her to be very confused. Apparently, after I had left, my mother solicited my younger brother for a ride to the doctors. On the way my mother turned to my brother and said "what concert are we going to?" My brother, horrified and confused at the situation, called our friends for help and went from there.

My mom spent a week in the hospital. After being put on fluids, she became more stable, but she wasn't getting strength back. By the end of the week the doctors presented us with two options.

We could attempt to start my mother on another round of chemo, or we could take her home on hospice. The doctor basically asked if we wanted to try putting my mom through more treatments, or send her home to pass away. That is not a question that my degree had prepared me for. People told me to be positive, there were solutions, but they hadn't seen what I had. My mother was wasting away. It felt almost cruel to try anything more rigorous than raising and lowering her bed or making her drink a bland protein shake, let alone pump her full of chemicals that had already made her so miserable (despite her best efforts at hiding it).

I went home with my mind swimming. Up until then, everything felt so up in the air. She had beat cancer before, so surely she could do it again? But at the same time, how many times can your body face such intensive treatments and situations without permanent and rapidly declining damage? It was then I remembered an odd call I had received the morning before my mom was sent to the hospital. My boyfriend at the time had called as I was waking up and asked if everything was alright. Confused, I confirmed that everything was as usual. On the island where he was from, dreaming about a wedding signified that someone was going to pass away very soon. He told me that he had a dream that I was getting married, but I was crying. I assured him everything was fine, and got ready for the day. As I thought back to that phone call, I cried for the first time since this whole ordeal had begun.

My mother signed the papers to return home the next morning, and passed away the day after returning home.

My mother was the closest to saintly that I think you could achieve in her position. Of course she wasn't perfect, but even her flaws just seemed to round out and compliment what a wonderful and humble human being she was. Her faith was incredibly important to her, and she held it with firmness and hope in her darkest times, as opposed to becoming bitter as many would feel justified in doing so. The only solace I can take from this is that if anyone is going to any sort of celebrated tier or destination in whatever after life there is, it will be her.

27 Weeks, 761 Grams, and 104 Days: On Redefining "Progress" and Accepting Loss

Erin Harrop

It's difficult to know where to begin when writing about death, dying, grief, and loss. This piece is about the grief and loss of my son's stay in the neonatal intensive care unit after he was born. Someone once asked me, why—if my son survived—did I talk so much about grief? Grief and loss do not always begin at a death; sometimes we grieve losses months or years before a person passes. Other times we grieve losses of expectations or lives that will never be lived. In reflecting on my son's lengthy stay in the neonatal intensive care unit, I have had to grieve the loss of a certain type of infancy and motherhood and accept a different one. Instead of spending infancy in a decorated nursery, with play dates, messy first foods, and baby snuggles, my son's infancy was one of hand sanitizer, wires, monitors, catheters, surgeries, alarms, and breast pumps.

It is a different experience to mother your child through a plastic box, unable to hold or bathe or nurse. And in that hygienic separation, there is safety—and grief.

I have wanted to be a mother most of my life, and up until I was 17 years old, I had wanted to be a midwife when I grew up. I can remember looking at my mother's books about pregnancy and fetal development on the bottom shelf of our bookshelf. I was fascinated by the pictures of tiny embryos and fetuses pictured in their pages— the little mitotic blackberry of cells attached to a uterine wall, the little tad-pole-ish, translucent fetus floating in amniotic fluid, the more infant-looking third-trimester fetus squished into the too-small womb. The fact that we humans start from a single cell, and grow into a whole complicated person fascinated me. As I took more biology and neurobiology classes when I got older, I was more impressed and dumb-founded by the whole process.

I had also looked forward to being pregnant. I had looked forward to seeing my body grow and change; I was curious what I would look like and how my body would shift. I looked forward to balancing a book or a plate on a big, round, stretched third-trimester belly. I wondered what my belly button would look like. I looked forward to having my partner feel the baby kick; I looked forward to seeing my belly move, see the baby roll, or maybe feel an elbow or a knee somewhere near my internal organs. I looked forward to feeling a transcendent, indescribable, innate sense of connection to the being I was growing inside me. I anticipated how I would respond to strangers who would touch my belly uninvited (I had wanted to touch their bellies as a retort). I looked forward to picking out a nice gender-neutral color for a nursery, and then assembling a crib (with some predictable frustration) with my partner. I wondered what it would feel like to have my breasts swell with milk and maybe leak through my shirt as my body prepared for the baby's arrival.

I was curious about where my water would break. I was curious about the struggle and pain of childbirth (How would I cope? What would it feel like? How close would I get to my breaking point?). I was looking forward to bonding with my partner in such an intimate, vulnerable, pressed-to-the-edge experience. I was looking forward to having my mother be my birth coach, as she had done for three other women before me. I was looking forward to the novel experience of birth. I wondered what it would be like to see my baby for the first time as he wiggled, and cried, covered in blood and fluid and that weird white waxy stuff on newborns' skin.

I wondered what it would feel like to have the baby placed on my chest after birth—would it be the best day of my life, the way so many people described the day their first child was born?

Would it change my life or at least alter my perspective? Would I shed tears of joy seeing this precious little human we created?

But these things did not happen. I had been so sick during my pregnancy that I had not been able to gain much weight. Many people didn't even know I was pregnant at the time I gave birth. I never got that basketball belly. My partner never got to feel the baby kick in the womb (well, he might have once, but we couldn't really tell for sure). My belly and breasts never swelled in anticipation; my water never broke—until the doctors punctured it. When my son was born, we had not painted the nursery or even picked out a crib (much less assembled it!). We had not even started our childbirth preparation class. My son was born during an emergency c-section.

My partner wasn't present when we started the procedure. I coded in response to the anesthesia.

When I coded, and the doctors came flooding through the doors, I thought my baby was dying. As I went out of consciousness, I remember thinking in a panic that my partner would hate the baby for the rest of his life, because I had died in childbirth, and I didn't want my son or partner to live with that burden.

But we survived that day. About 10 hours after Jason was born, I got to see him for the first time. He was tiny and translucent, with closed eyes, in a clear, heated box, with wires and tubes all over him. He didn't care that I was there; I felt no transcendent, indescribable, innate sense of connection to him. He looked like a fetus, and I guess technically, he was. Jason was born at 27 weeks, and 761 grams (1lb 11oz). Life was tenuous at first; we didn't know what would happen from one day to the next.

For the first several days, it was hard to be at his bedside, because he kept requiring resuscitation, and it was hard to hear the alarms go off, see the nurses rush in, and watch as his tiny body was palpitated to stimulate his heart. Maybe it was hard for me to feel connected, because I was afraid to hope, and I didn't want to feel the profoundness of loss that comes when you deeply love someone who passes.

Connection grew slowly. We started to celebrate different landmarks. Instead of anticipating his first smile or his first cry, we had different measures of progress. After 2 days, I pumped one whole milliliter of breast-milk (that amounts to several drops); after 7 days, I pumped 30 mils. Within a week, I could pump enough to feed him. After 10 days, I got to hold him for the first time. After 11 days, he finally pooped, confirming that his anus was, in fact, connected to his colon (we were uncertain for a while). After 14 days, he was taken off the ventilator. After 21 days, he got his first bath. After 6 weeks, he was finally big enough for a tiny preemie onesie. After 85 days, he weaned off of his respiratory support. At 103 days, he fed by mouth for 24 hours. After 104 days, we finally got to go home.

In the NICU, we were constantly adjusting our expectations and hopes. He would get better some weeks, and sicker others; we had no assurances of the type of life Jason would have if he survived; chronic illnesses and disabilities are common among 27-weekers. It was hard to hear people vaguely state that "everything would work out," because it might not. And it didn't help when well-intentioned people told me how "this was all a part of God's will," or that "God had us covered," because covered or not, babies fucking die sometimes (I think this was the anger stage of grief). I rebelled when people called him a "little fighter," because I just wanted him to be a baby—no fighting required. The first time I accidentally called him a "little trooper" after one of his surgeries, I broke down and cried.

I envied every pregnant woman with a giant belly that I saw; I wanted the swollen feet and sore back she was complaining about. I cringed when people said, "I don't care what gender the baby is, as long as it's healthy." Because sometimes, babies aren't healthy. And that doesn't make them any less loved or any less of a blessing. Today, Jason is a fun, mischievous, observant, problem-solving 2-year-old; he has several residual health issues from his prematurity. I wouldn't call him "healthy" or "normal," and we are all blessed. And not every story continues like this; many parents leave NICUs with an empty car seat sitting at home, unopened in its box.

Much of my grief process around my son's birth has been in grieving expectations, and anticipating a death that (graciously) did not come. Looking back, I think I looked forward to the things I did (a big belly, holding hands with my partner during birth, etc.) partly because of my own interests and fascinations and desires, and partly because of what I had been socialized to believe about "womanhood" and "mothering." In that socialization, there isn't much room for things to go differently. There is only room for small variations (an epidural vs. a natural birth or a cesarean vs. a vaginal delivery), but not big ones. This process has expanded my ideas of what it means to parent. I think less about "bottle vs. breast" or "home births vs. hospitals", and much more about how to be present with my son, hold his pain (and my own), and enjoy all the small, sweet, remarkable moments I get with him. As I reflect on his first few months outside the womb, I prefer not to invalidate the good I have experienced by regretting that this ever happened.

However, I also honor the difficulty and grief inherent in the process. So, this piece is a tribute to the things that went really unexpectedly differently in Jason's birth story, and how I have been coping with the aftermath.

I Feel So Very Broken

Sharon Ehlers

I feel so very broken
So very alone
My whole world has changed
My heart feels like stone
I desperately miss you
Since you went away
I can't find the words
There's no more I can say

WHEN DEATH COMES

Ann Lovejoy

When my mother died, it was between two blinks of an eye. No labored Cheyne-Stokes breathing.

No gasp, no moan, no sigh. Just a soundless slipping away while my back was turned to put down the warm wash cloth I'd used to gently wipe her face. She'd lingered painfully until the arrival of my oldest brother set her free. Though she'd been mostly unresponsive for the past few days, Tim sang hymns and talked with her all the day before and she slept more peacefully that night than she had in a long time. In the morning, she didn't open her eyes when I told her I was taking Tim to the ferry so he could get to the airport, but she squeezed my hand a little bit. I was gone less than an hour and she was resting quietly when I got home.

As I'd been doing for days now, I used a dampened sponge swab to clean her mouth and rubbed a little honey chapstick on her dry lips. The washcloth sat in a bowl of warm water so it wouldn't cool off too much before I needed it. I wiped the grainy sleep from her eyes and the sticky drool from her chin. I turned to put down the cloth and when I turned back, she was gone. Or so I thought. I wasn't sure what to do so I got a hand mirror and sure enough, no mist on the mirror. A fleeting thought made me almost smile through slow tears: no mist on the mirror-great song title?

The room that had been so full for so long seemed empty in a new way. I called hospice and said, "I think my mom just died but I'm not completely sure." I was assured that a nurse would be on her way as soon as she finished up with another family. No hurry, I said.

The doorbell rang and a friend stood at the door. "I brought you some cheese," he said, offering a round of homemade goat cheese. I thanked him and said, "I think my mom just died but I'm not sure" again. Stephen said, "Well, let's go see." We walked the few steps to the hospital bed and Stephen lifted Mom's arm, then let it drop. "Yes, I think she's dead," he said. "Shall we pray?"

Stephen said "Lord, we commend Jean's spirit into your care and ask for the blessing of comfort for those who loved her." Then he went home. At that time, Stephen was undergoing treatment for the cancer that would kill him a few years later and although he was calm and steady while looking death in the face, he clearly needed some alone time.

I called my kids, who had been helping me take care of Mom for several years now. I called my brothers, who were already on the ferry, heading for my house. I'd told everyone that the time was definitely drawing near and they had decided to come vigil with me.

My daughter in love was the first one on the scene. Seven months pregnant and with a two year old in her arms, Kate hugged me warmly and suggested we get Mom cleaned up. My little grandson looked at me and burst into tears, saying "Goodbye, Granny!" Kate reassured him that I wasn't dying, but my mother, his GG. "Oh," he said, wiping off his tears. "Granny, will you read me a story?"

Kate and I washed Mom, put on the last clean nappy she'd ever need, and put on her favorite nightgown, soft as a cloud. We'd take to dressing her in T-shirts split down the back just under the neckband. Soft and simple, these let us change her clothes with as little disturbance as possible, but now, silly as it seemed, I wanted to give her the comfort of that fleece gown.

I lit candles and set them around the room, once my own, now given over to Mom's needs. When she could no longer live "alone" (not counting the nearly 24-7 caregivers, mostly family and friends), I emptied my bedroom suite and filled it with Mom's favorite furniture and paintings. I slept on a little daybed in my sunroom, with a glass door between us.

I sat in my old rocker, gift from a dear friend who died too soon. I kept thinking about Mary Oliver's poem:

when death comes
like an iceberg between the shoulder blades,
I want to step through the door full of curiosity,
wondering:
what is it going to be like, that cottage of darkness?

Coda

Donna James

Agitated on the edge of a railed bed
replacing the sofa that cushioned
years of conjugal conversation,
you sit awake a day and a night;
your mind awash in toxins
a tumor won't let your liver remove.
The hospice nurse prescribes a quadruple dose
to calm you into sleep. I come to you.
Your eyes close as your head surrenders to my hand.
Open, I say to your upturned face.
Mother and chick, your mouth opens wide,
I slip the syringe under your tongue.
I bid you,
Close.
One push, god Morpheus enshrouds
you fall from my breast
in his clutch.
I don't know yet—these words
are our last.

22 Hours

Linda Shadwell Hart

Along with losing Greg, the way and time it took in the end remains to me almost unbelievable.

Greg feared old age and didn't even have a primary care doc at the time of his death. He crammed something "worthwhile" into every day and at age 66 with advanced cancer was still bicycle commuting, skiing black diamond runs, and moving 2 man boulders. The beginning of the end was a spontaneous fracture of his right humerus while just twisting a top off a bottle. In that moment we knew. Death had broken through the ramparts.

Greg was raised in the Catholic Church and had considered himself a "recovered Catholic" for decades. I worked at a local hospital for many years before it was bought by Catholic Health Initiatives and vehemently oppose any faith based imposition into health care, especially around reproductive rights for women and the Death With Dignity Act. When it was time to have hospice come into our home we learned it was through CHI. All I could say is "Fuck, the Catholics are coming." But ultimately, "The Catholics" served us well.

8:30 pm, on May 20th 2017, a hospice nurse called us in the evening to check on Greg. He had developed a new pain in his esophagus that made it hard to eat. We had spoken with them several times over those few days, trying different remedies geared for heartburn. We weren't expecting what the nurse would tell us. The hospice doctor had pulled and read through all of Greg's records and based on his symptoms that didn't respond to typical treatment, the timing and location of his most recent radiation treatment, the nurse stated, "The doctor is certain that what you are experiencing is a radiation burn to your esophagus. This will develop into an ulcer and you will have massive uncontrollable bleeding. You will die from this, and it will be unstoppable." She urged us to leave immediately for the nearest emergency department where they could at least sedate Greg and manage his airway as the blood came. There was no cure, only a refuge that could help us cope with the bloody end. Could be 1 hour, 5 hours or 5 days...but the end was in sight, and nothing could turn back the red tide. "Get out dark towels...dark towels, lots of them... there will be a lot of blood," the nurse said.

I am an ER nurse and have seen people "bleed out". I knew exactly what that looked like.

We didn't want Greg to die on an ER gurney. He was snug and comfy in his soft recliner chair in our home. The home he built and loved.

"We have the Death With Dignity cocktail...are you telling us it is time to make that decision?"

"Yes...." was her reply. Calm. Clear.

We quickly called our family and Greg made a wild last post to his *Caring Bridge* page. Then, Greg just let down. I think all the medications he took for pain rallied once his will to fight diminished. He quickly fell into a deep sleep. Within the hour our children were here and we woke him to take the pre-medication (Reglan) for the Death With Dignity cocktail. We were all about 6 inches from his face when he asked what the med was for.

9:30 p.m. May 20th.

"Wake up, Honey, take this medicine."

"What is this for?"

"It's for nausea."

"I'm not nauseated"

"It is part of the cocktail"

"Oh, we're doing that now?"

"Yes, Dad."

It hurt to swallow, but he got the pill down, smiled warmly at all of us, and immediately fell back to sleep.

10:30 p.m.

"Wake up Greg, you need to drink this"

Greg was hard to wake up. We were again, all three of us, six inches from his face.

"Wake up, Dad"

"You need to drink this" 'This'...was four ounces of a bitter, lime green slurry.

"What is this for?"

"It's the cocktail, Dear. You have to drink it now."

"Oh, we're doing this now?"

"Yes, honey. You have to. Right now."

Greg lifted the cup to his lips and barely tasted it before he struck his arm out with the cup and turned his head away..

"No...I can't drink this...it's horrible."

Everyone's eyes widened. Fueled with the fear that this burn in his esophagus could blow at any time and Greg would die suffocating on a garden hose emission of blood coming up his throat, we all inched in closer...

"Dad!"

"Honey"

"You have got to drink this right now!"

It was a horrible moment, but with continued coaxing Greg stayed awake and worked through his bitter drink.

"keep going"

"drink the last of it"

"all of it"

In true Greg fashion, his black humor still intact, with the three of us still inches from his face, he did a credible rendition of Linda Blair in that well known scene from the Exorcist... he rolled his eyes back, let out a howl and twisted his head as far around as he could. We all jumped back and he broke into his uncontrollable belly laugh. He continued laughing so hard he was holding his stomach.

"God dammit, Dad!!"

"Greg!"

He laughed harder. His chuckle finally subsided, and he closed his eyes with a smile, and that "aha! gotcha!" look of fun and contentment over his face. He never woke again.

"Will it be soon?" our children asked.

"Will it work before the ulcer breaks open?" I tried to reassure them, as I grappled with the same question.

May 21st, 0230. I added Fentanyl patches on his torso. They had always worked more quickly on him then what the directions indicated.

0630 With the love of a wife, and the knowledge of a nurse, I listened to and evaluated every breath Greg took. Was it even... had it slowed... was it shallow or full... were the intervals spacing out...

18 breaths a minute

full, even, unlabored.

A normal respiratory pattern.

Thus began the vigorous support to "treat the pain" and out race the Reaper.

Knowing Greg needed additional medication to get him to the other side, we called the hospice nurse for more a more concentrated form of pain medication.

She insisted on coming to see him before sending a prescription to the pharmacy.

The young nurse came and looked at Greg, deep asleep with a look of peace on his face. The Catholics are committed to treating pain at the end of life, not assisted suicide.

I wept as I tried to convince her that he looked peaceful now but had bouts of waking with pain and anxiety.

0900. Greg's (very Catholic) 90 year old mother and sister arrived. We had tried to spare her from the knowledge that Greg would take his own life at his chosen time. Greg's mom is also a retired nurse.

At shorter and shorter intervals, I continued to medicate Greg with the concentrated morphine the hospice nurse finally got for us. "What are you giving him?" his mother asked, quietly, from her look-out post on the couch near her son.

"Morphine," I replied.

30 minutes later:

"What are you giving him now?"

"Ativan"

And so it went. Until 8:30 that night.

May 21st, 22 hours after drinking "the green lizard," Greg drew his last breath. His children, his sister, and I, the ones who fearlessly faced down the reaper to help Greg have a comfortable death in his favorite chair, in his own home, finally drew a full breath.

Up Every Night

Sharon Ehlers

I am up every night
I can't close my eyes
I am afraid if I do
I'll remember the goodbye
How the world has so changed
More than I wanted it to
With you no longer here
I'm not sure what to do

Near the End

Alison Eckels

Near the end
you might feel as if you are entering new territory.

And in a moment,
shorter or longer depending on your journey,
you might realize that you recognize this place,
that you have known it all along,
known it was there just on the other side of the veil.

In the midst of The Busy Years
this may seem far away, non-existent, unreal.
But it is always there,
just as the stars are in the sky
even when the sun bathes the side of the planet we are on.

Near the end,
we are near the beginning.
This truth can be wonderful and terrifying
all at the same time.

But we have crossed many endings and beginnings along our way.

We have practiced transitions,
made it through them again and again.

Listen for the music.

The stars are singing.

You are loved.

AFTER

FOREVER IS NOT LONG ENOUGH

Amy Ferris

From Grief Dialogues Founder Elizabeth Coplan:

"One of my favorite writers is Amy Ferris, who, to me, is a dead-ringer for Meryl Streep, and I mean that in the best way. Amy's ability to write words both brief and profound on so many different and serious topics blows me away each time I read them.

When I read Amy's post on her Facebook page, I did more than simply like the post or even give it a Wow or a Heart emoji. I messaged her and asked her permission to post her story about a BFF and her dying husband. Amy replied: "Yes, please post." I share this with you here exactly how it is published on My Alzheimer's Story. It is also published on Amy's Blog."

There is an interfaith chapel at the New York-Presbyterian/Weill Cornell Hospital.

My best girl's husband is very ill. Intensive care. I drove her into the city so she can be with him, kiss him, smooth his hair and look into his eyes and tell him how much she loves him; to hold his hand and watch him sleep. She couldn't bear driving into the city, she hadn't slept last night, and who wants to drive all alone for two fucking hours – 4 roundtrip – in traffic while your mind is racing all over the crazy-ass place.

I told her today it would be just like a girls day out, except, you know, without all the fun and the wine. That sounds peachy, she said, with an extra side of sarcasm.

I left them alone in his hospital room, while I moseyed on over to a fancy schmancy nail salon on the upper east side and told the mani-pedicurist to please, please, massage my feet for at least seven hours. So much nervous laughter; she had no idea if I was serious. And, why would she? I settled: 20 minutes and a pedicure. Heaven. Or for now, close enough.

My friend texted me: a half-hour more, please? She wanted a half hour more with him. To wash his face, and feed him some food, and you know, more time.

Of course.

More time.

Who doesn't want that.

I found myself sitting in the interfaith chapel. A place I never go into, never wander into. Ever. I sat in a row by the exit door. Four men – all muslim – kneeling on prayer rugs in the front of the chapel, praying in unison, as if it were perfectly choreographed. A beautiful black woman, impeccably dressed, across the aisle, her eyes prayer closed as she held onto – grasped – the cameo pendant around her neck. Two jewish women, maybe, possibly, a mother and a daughter, sitting a few rows in front of me, their heads slowly nodding, bobbing, speaking hushed words I couldn't understand. A young white boy, a just turned teenager, his body rubbing up against the wall, as he fought back tears. A stained glass mandala, massive carved candle-sticks, Giacometti-esque figures, a long narrow altar table draped with starch linen. Just the right touches. A small intimate room for personal prayers.

I closed my eyes, I thought of my friend, his joy full big life, his now battle, his massive bravery. All of that became my prayer. I thought of my gorgeous friend; her heart, her worries, her fears, her deep uncluttered and unconditional love for him; all of that became my prayer. I thought of Ken and his health and his worries and his uneasiness about showing, revealing, his frailty and how that keeps him more to himself and that became my prayer; I thought of some friends who I haven't seen or spoken to in a while, and how in that moment, that exact moment, in that chapel I knew they were etched deep in my heart and nothing could or would change that and that became my prayer, and I thought of my mom and dad and I tried to imagine them together as I squinted real hard conjuring them up in my minds eye, and how on some days I longed for them and that thought led to my brother, and to my entire family, a family that is no longer, and for a few long unplanned moments I travelled from anger to resentment to sadness to peace, and as I stopped trying to imagine their faces, I began to wish them well and that became my prayer.

You can hear a pin drop.

And I thought about this world, our world, and the black woman praying across from me as she grasped her cameo pendant, and the young white boy velcro-ed to the wall, his bottom lip quivering; and the muslim men deep in prayer, and the jewish women reciting something under their collective breath while they now held hands, and we were all, no doubt, silently offering up our fears and our worries and our heartache and our greatest doubts and deep need for hope and comfort and ease and love, and rekindling – doubling up – on promises once made, somehow forgotten or lost, and bartering with the Universe or God or deities or cameos or Netflix or Jon Stewart or whoever you call it; bartering in hopes that what we offer up – exchange – will add more years more days more weeks more months – more time – enough time to make good, to say I'm sorry, enough time to admit fuck ups and fuck downs and fuck offs, enough time to mend misunderstandings, miscommunications; some scattered misfortune; enough time to say – ad nauseam, I might add – I can't fucking live without you; enough time to love more, to love better, to get love right, to do it right; enough time to say I won't let you go so fast; not so fucking fast. I got you.

In that chapel on this day with death circling every floor; the absolute take away: forever is not long enough.

You are so right, Amy, you are so right!

IN THE RIVER OUSE

Mike Cordle

Morticians and medical examiners
tell of the horror,
or sad moment of silent respect,
or emptiness of heart they feel
when they must turn over the body
of a not too lately deceased
from the back side to the front side,
and the body heaves a sigh.

That sigh.
I have not heard it.
But I have imagined it.
I have practiced heaving sighs.
All my life I have practiced heaving sighs,
noting how some last longer and some hurt more,
how some say more, and some say nothing.

East of Seattle,
At the top of Mount Si
I have seen rivers and streams
I wonder if the mountain sighs
or the rivers do.

Like I do. Like the overturned bodies do.

Do those rivers flow life and death?
Virginia Woolf filled her pockets with stones and sighs
and walked into the River Ouse
which I am told by some
is pronounced ooze.

Those bodies on the metal tables
of morticians and medical examiners:
their bottoms go flat and uncomely,
like an airless tire on a tractor.

Supple no more,
empty of the resistance and resilience of
blood and fat filled cells.
No more sitting up on the butt,
instead, the body is given over to
disappearing,
like the last breath of that last sigh.

A Psalm for Leona at Old Faithful

Mary Langer Thompson

I've traveled a long way to sit before you,
to witness your faithfulness
near Heart Lake on the map.
I passed fawns frolicking at roadside,
crossed rumble strips and saw
"No Services" Sunday signs.

Lately, my God is not predictable,
and like with you, I can't get close.
So today I need you to be my American Lourdes.

How can this happen to a child? We are gobsmacked.
My tears have been building up. I need release.
So, you Old Geyser, shoot your burning liquid.
Scald God to get his attention.
Make Him drink and Godsmack her with healing.

Do your waterworks, Old Faithful.
Make even the stones cry out her name.

Creating the Last Conversation with My Deceased Brother

Robyn Faust Gabe, PhD

If I had the chance to say goodbye: an imagined conversation at my brother's grave.

My brother unexpectedly died in his sleep 12 years ago. Our last conversation was the day of my wedding and we had had a verbal disagreement. That night, my brother had several more disagreements with friends and family, along with being blatantly drunk. It has always bothered me that I never got the chance to say goodbye to him. I struggled with guilt for a long time. I decided to go to his grave and have a conversation with him. I pretended that I knew he was dying from a kidney disorder and we had one last chance to speak. The conversation in my head went something like this:

Robyn: Do you have any regrets?

Eric: Yes, that I didn't beat up certain people that deserved it.

Robyn: Oh? So your biggest regret is not beating up people?

Eric: Yeah. That, and never getting to beat you in a cooking challenge.

Robyn: What are you talking about? Your smoked ribs and fried turkey are wonderful!

Eric: But you can make chicken parm and stuffed shells and other fancy dishes.

Robyn: So, I can teach you.

Eric: There's no time.

Robyn: We can make time.

Eric: No, you just got married and bought a house. You have your own life to live .

Robyn: Just because I no longer live with mom and dad, does not mean our relationship is over.

Eric: It might, because you are the golden child who will give them a grandchild.

Robyn: You sound jealous.

Eric: Always. We have competed for years.

Robyn: I know. I've always felt that dad favored you more than me.

Eric: And I felt that mom favored you more than me, but that I was able to manipulate her, which really pissed you off.

Robyn: Yes it did, you could get anything you wanted out of her. And they would always watch your practices, and help you with your school work.

Eric: I wasn't smart and independent like you.

Robyn: Look at us, back to being jealous and bickering.

Eric: Yes, it's exhausting.

Robyn: Let's talk about something else.

Eric: Okay.

Robyn: How about what makes you happy?

Eric: Smoking meat and designing cars.

Robyn: You could make a career out of either one.

Eric: Actually, I have an interview at an exotic car designer in Miami. I think I got the job already, because they already have my vette design on their website.

Robyn: Great! You must be so happy.

Eric: I was, I mean, I am. But...I finally get my dream job when my life will be cut short.

Robyn : What do you mean?

Eric: I'm dying from a rare kidney complication.

Robyn: Come again?

Eric: I have fetal lobulations of the kidney.

Robyn: I have no idea what that is, but let's see if I am a kidney match.

Eric: It means my kidneys never separated at birth and I have one child size kidney. No - I do not want one of your kidneys.

Robyn : You are 23 years old and are just finding out about this now!

Eric : It's a shock to me too. People will think I destroyed my organs from the way I drink, eat, and use drugs.

Robyn: This is crazy, there has to be something that I can do?

Eric: Take care of mom and dad. They won't be able to cope with my death.

Robyn: What about me, who is going to take care of me?

Eric: You are strong, and will be able to take care of all three of you. I need to go to sleep now. I will not wake up.

Robyn: But I have so much more to say to you!

Eric: It will have to wait, until we see each other again. Good-bye. I love you.

Eric was 23 years old, when he died in his sleep. Six months later when we received the autopsy report, we found out about his kidney condition. I have always been dumbfounded that his condition was never discovered. I knew he was born with jaundice and had to stay in the hospital for a few extra days. I also knew he'd failed the blood test to obtain a certain acne medication as a teenager. Lastly, I knew his wrists were yellowish, along with his lower back, and he had a prescription for blood tests that was sitting on his dresser. Instead, he choose to fill the medication without first undergoing the blood tests. Maybe they would have showed issues with kidney function? I will never know.

Though this conversation never happened, the thought of how it would have gone has brought me comfort. The comfort stems from knowing that my brother never would have accepted one of my kidneys, even if we were a match. He was petrified of hospitals. He had an immense distrust for the medical field, which is probably why he never followed through with the blood tests. I still regret not trying to interfere more with his life, but I knew how he would shut people out when he did not want to have a certain discussion. I still think of him every day and still miss him every day. He will always have a place in my heart.

WE PRAY

Will Silverman

We pray
We take
We wait
For the fire
To burn
We learn
In turn
To curb desire
We judge
Too much
Don't trust
In each other
The storm
Takes form
We're warned
But fail
to discover
Recall
Your soul
Take hold
Of this moment
We breathe
We grieve
We leave
No hope for atonement
We cry
Goodbye
Blanched sky
Melts into horizon
With no
Remorse
Changed course
In deafening silence
We die

I am a Marionette

Megan Vered

"Mom, I'm bored."

"Go play with your sister."

"She's boring."

"Go read a book."

"I already did."

"Then draw a picture."

"My crayons are broken."

Geh shlog zich kop en vant. (Literal translation: "Go bang your head against the wall.")

This is only one example of the Yiddish disciplinary tactics employed by my mother when we were kids. Yiddish was Mom's first language. She was not even exposed to English until she went to kindergarten. Yiddish was also the secret language that my grandparents reverted to when they did not want us to understand them. We caught on fast and learned to crack the code. We knew that *gib a cook* meant "take a look"; that *gay gezunte hate* meant "go in good health"; that *tsorris* was "suffering." And, of course, my grandmother bathed us in Yiddish endearments that were well understood: *shayna meydela, shayna velt, shayna mamela* (literal translations: beautiful maiden, beautiful world, beautiful little mother).

I am bruised, not just by my mother's death, but also by the passing of the Yiddish language and the first generation American-Jewish experience. Ancient voices spoke to me through my mother's flesh. Her presence kept me linked to her history and the heartbeat of my ancestors. Encircled by the reverberation of past life experiences, I gained comfort and strength. Now that she is gone, precious ties have been severed.

I am a marionette whose strings have been dropped. Not that Mom controlled my every move like some manic puppeteer, but her presence was a lifeline that kept me linked to those who came before. Without her I feel rootless, lifeless. When I move my arm to gesture to a stranger or lift my leg to walk, there is nothing holding me in place. I am in free fall with no point of reference. No one to slip an arm through mine and keep me linked to tradition, ritual, custom.

Mom's Yiddish expressions—vibrant word salads—both entertained and annoyed. She held high expectations that I would rise to the occasion and be a good sport. When I complained about life being unfair, her stock response was, "I never promised you a rose garden." When my grousing persisted, she said, "I'll thank you to keep a civil tongue in your mouth, young lady." When I persevered with no end in sight, she switched to Yiddish.

Gay hack mir nisht kan chinik. (Literal translation: "Don't bang me a teakettle," as in "stop nudging me!")

I can also hear her voice of derision when she would see something in a store that was too kitschy: *Ach, so ongepatshket!* (Literal translation: "Too fussy.")

The word *ferblunjit* was used when she was feeling "at sixes and sevens" or out of sorts. (Literal translation: "Mixed up and lost.")

When we sneezed, a *Zay gezunt* was bestowed for the first three sneezes. (Literal translation: "To your health.")

Sneeze number four, however, invoked, *Gay en drered du krigst shein a kalt.* (Literal translation: "Into the earth with you already; you're getting a cold.")

When we did good, Mom would *kvell*; when we did her proud, she would *shep naches*; when we were bad, she'd cry, *gay avek*.

Without the melody of my mother's song, my strength falters. No wall of wisdom to push against so that I can rebound. I have lost all ricochet power. And without the strings that have kept me tethered to Mom's story, my life appears flat, one-dimensional. And on top of this, I am guilty of dropping the ancestral ball, having never used Yiddish expressions with my own children with the exception of the occasional *oy vey*.

As we grew older and our children matured, Mom's Yiddishisms shifted to expressions of grandmotherly endearment.

Ahz m'lebt der lebt mir. (Literal translation: "If you live long enough, you will live to see it happen.")

Mishugeneh ganz, mashugeneh griben. (Literal translation: "Crazy geese, crazy goslings.")

I am a marionette whose strings have gone slack. I forget birthdays and punch lines and how our family first met certain friends. Lose track of bloodlines and which cousins are on which side of the family. I look at photographs and cannot decipher whether the girl next to me in the photo is an elementary school friend or my next door neighbor's sister. What will bring me back to life now that Mom is gone? Who will repeat the stories to me with such care and precision? An entire civilization is heaving its final, inconsolable breath.

I search through boxes of mementos for reassurance that I will not lose sight of my ancestral footprint. In among the greeting cards and photographs I find lined paper, folded in thirds. A four-page summary of her lineage, her first generation American-Jewish experience in her perfectly appointed handwriting. I take a deep breath and say *thank you*.

I dream one night after Mom's death that she is crying. She tells me that she is feeling undone. "You mean *ferblunjit*, Mom?" I tell her that I am a marionette who has lost her strings. "We make a fine pair," I say.

For weeks, I sob myself into a stupor before falling asleep. Each wave of tears evokes another level of loss. Who would ever love me the way my mother did? Who would hold my strings with such tenacity? Who would *kvell* over my every triumph no matter how small? She knew every soppy detail of my life story. The name of every boy I ever loved, every girl who turned against me. She was the one who soothed me through the endless falling outs and rapprochements with my younger sister. Who else would ever be so enchanted by the tiny particles of my life? And who else but my mother would tell me to bang my head against the wall?

GONE

Aspen Drake

When I was little and the world was quiet,
I would lie in bed and think about the earth
and how big it was.

Then my mind would shift to the solar system,
and how we are constantly floating around amongst
other planets and countless stars.

I would think about how there was even more beyond that,
perhaps beyond anything a single person could
imagine.

I would begin to feel dizzy, and would have to roll
over and consider something on a smaller scale.
That's how I would describe losing my mother.

It's something that I know happened, but it's not something I
take time to regularly consider.
And when I do, it's weird as f@#k.

And despite how big the world is, with all its winding roads
and hidden places I haven't visited
And how many launches we are making into space,

My mom isn't there.
I won't find her anywhere. Not around the corner of a noisy
street market like in some art film.

Not on another planet that we'll eventually colonize like some
sci-fi twist.
She's gone.

Hospice: A Love Story

Elizabeth Coplan

CHARACTERS

ANNE   A woman in her early 60s
BETSY   A woman in her early 50s

SETTING

A Catholic church confessional and a therapist office

PROPS

A prayer kneeling bench, a chair, St. Patrick's Day balloon (slightly deflated), downloaded music box version of It's a Small World

TIME

The present

AT RISE: On one side of the stage is a couch. On the other is a prayer kneeling bench. Music plays.)

(Betsy enters carrying a deflated St. Patrick's Day balloon. Knocks on an imaginary door. Ties balloon to couch leg. Anne enters. Knocks on a different imaginary door. Anne opens door. Kneels on prayer bench.)

ANNE
(makes Sign of Cross)
Bless me Father for I have sinned. It has been 42 years since my last confession.

BETSY
(Lies on sofa)
Sorry I have missed a few appointments Doctor.

ANNE

Yes, well, I'm here, so let's make the most of it.
I'm supposed to be sorry for my sins, right? Guess I
should have Googled the topic.
(A moment)

ANNE/BETSY (unison)

I killed my mother.

ANNE

And for that I am truly sorry. (Beat) No, I'm not truly
sorry. God abandoned her. There was no God in that
room.
Oh God, I never should have come. I don't remember
how to do this confession thing. When I was younger I
kept a list of my sins taped to the back of my bed-
room door.
Just so I would have something to say to the priest.
Of course I wrote down things like I sassed my mother.
Three times. After my sister was born I wrote I had
anger and lust. At least 7 times. One lust for each
day of the week. I remember the nuns taught us lust
meant thoughtlessness and self-love.
They never said anything about sex or adultery.
Apparently sex and adultery were considered the adult
version of "lust." All I cared about was getting rid
of my interloper sister. And goddamn my sister. Mom
was in excruciating pain.

BETSY

Dr. Turner, I didn't actually kill Mom. But I helped.
No, I didn't help so I killed my mother.

ANNE

I wasn't really going to kill her but all was lost.

BETSY

My sister Anne was making all the decisions about
Mom's health care and when to bring in Hospice. All
she talked about was giving Mom the morphine. I think…

ANNE/BETSY (unison)

I/Anne just wanted to get on with her/my life.

ANNE

Then my sister asks our mom,

ANNE/BETSY (unison)

"Do you want to die?"

ANNE

Of all the idiotic questions. How the hell was she
supposed to answer? You had already performed the
Last Rites, Father. The Church would never forgive her
if she said "yes, let's hurry it up" or "I've changed
my mind."

(A moment)

My sister was always doing stupid stuff. I remember
the time we got Skipper dolls for Christmas. Betsy
cut her doll's hair. Tells me in her sickly sweet,
3-year-old voice "Skipper's hair will grow back." Oh,
the look on Betsy's face when I said…

ANNE/BETSY (unison)

It would never grow back.

ANNE

Is there a statute of limitations on what I confess?
Because I should add I was kinda mean to my sister

when she was little. You see, all I would do is yell
MOM! And then all Mom would do was yell "BETSY" and
my little sister would run…back to her room…in tears.
Mom just assumed I was right and Betsy was wrong. My
poor sister. I don't know why I did it. Because she
wasn't really bothering me. It was a lie.

(A moment)

I also lied this week Father. You see, Betsy made me
agree I would not give Mom any more morphine.

BETSY

We were supposed to go to Disneyland. All three of us.
That was the plan anyway. We loved all the fantasy and
the rides and the silliness. Thought it would make us
forget about Mom's illness. She was in remission you
see. But then her cancer came back.

We still joked about going because it was "on the cal-
endar." Mom lived and died by the calendar. Oh god, I
can't believe I said that!

(A moment)

I saw Mom's face, a tear on her cheek, her hands
clenched. You know, it's not fair. She lived a healthy
life. I didn't want to see her in pain, but I felt by
giving her morphine, we were hastening her death. We
were giving up on her.

ANNE

I told Betsy to give it up. Give up trying to make
sense of all it.

BETSY

One day we went out to buy groceries. The local farmer
was selling strawberries and I bought a carton. Mom
smelled them the moment we walked through the door.

184

So I fed her strawberries. Well, one strawberry. I cut
it in quarters and fed it to her.

ANNE

Betsy gave Mom a strawberry but she spit it out. It
left a stain on the white sheets. The sheets smelled.
It was gross.

ANNE/BETSY (unison)

We never/always changed her sheets.

BETSY

I tried to make her comfortable.

(A moment)

She liked this balloon I bought her. Flowers die so I
got her a balloon instead. She isn't (beat) wasn't Irish
but the choices were "Get Well," "Happy Birthday," or
"It's A Boy." Couldn't find "Speedy Death."

ANNE/BETSY (unison)

Oh god, we were so tired.

BETSY

Anne decided to lay out in the backyard. She said the
sun would feel good on her back. Guess she fell asleep
because the next door neighbor called. She thought
Anne was dead. Said she watched her for over 20 min-
utes and Anne never moved a muscle.

ANNE

When Betsy woke me up, I rubbed my face. The arti-
ficial turf left an imprint on my cheek and it hurt.

(A moment)

Father, I did not kill my mother because I wanted to go to Disneyland. I killed her because she was dying.

(A moment)

Sometimes when Mom was in a lot of pain, we did sit-ups.

ANNE/BETSY (unison)

Yes, sit-ups.

ANNE/BETSY (unison)

Mom loved/hated them.

ANNE

It was a funny little routine Betsy and I did. Betsy climbed on the back of the hospital bed. I climbed over the guardrail into the bed, and faced Mom. Then Anne crawled up the back of the bed and pushed Mom forward while I pulled Mom towards me. We then lowered her down. And I would back out of the bed. Always got my leg stuck in the bed rail and…

ANNE/BETSY (unison)

Mom laughed.

BETSY

Anne looked silly.

ANNE

When Mom laughed it reminded me of the time Betsy wore her Batman costume to church. Betsy wasn't Batgirl or even Catwoman; she was Batman.

ANNE/BETSY (unison)

The nuns loved her/me.

ANNE

Yes, they loved my sister. She was the cute one. The creative one.

BETSY

Anne was the smart one. Good grades. Loved to read. Liked to go out for tea and little sandwiches with Mom and pretend she was all sophisticated.

ANNE/BETSY (unison)

Mom liked her best.

ANNE

Betsy made those adorable Mother's Day cards from scratch. She'd even write her own "I Love Mom" poem. I spent 50 cents on a Hallmark card.

BETSY

Mom and Anne were alike in so many ways. For one, they both liked tea shops. I liked McDonald's. I had one of the very first Big Mac's.

ANNE

You should have seen my little sister. We called her...well, it's no longer politically correct, but we called her our Blond-headed Messkin. (Mexican)

BETSY

Mom designed paper dolls for Anne when she was little.

ANNE

Our mom made the cutest flowery dresses for my sister. I got the bright red, empire-waist, tent dress. I looked like a popsicle!

ANNE/BETSY (unison)

I love my sister. How do I tell her I killed our mother?

ANNE

I just gave Mom the prescribed dose of morphine.

ANNE/BETSY (unison)

I didn't like seeing her in pain.

ANNE

I tried to talk about something else, so I asked Betsy "When we go to Disneyland, what's the first place you want to go?"

BETSY

Then Anne started talking about Disneyland again! I couldn't believe it! And then out of my mouth comes "A Small World, I want to go to A Small World." I even started humming it. (hums) And then Mom smiled.

ANNE

Father, I appreciate your patience with me. Mom always said …

ANNE/BETSY (unison)

When it came to the Catholic Church we girls should just take what we want and leave the rest.

BETSY

I have so many regrets. Death is so complicated and there are many unanswered questions. Questions we never thought to ask.

ANNE

I have no regrets, Father. Oh, there were things I would have done differently in my life. For one thing, I would try to end Mom's pain sooner. But I have no regrets.

BETSY

Anyway…just as Mom was falling asleep…

ANNE/BETSY

… when Betsy/Anne turned her back, I gave Mom more morphine.

(A long moment)

ANNE

"It's okay Mom," I said. "Sleep well." Then Mom (Beat)

BETSY

(Beat) fell asleep.

(LIGHTS FADE SLOWLY. Music plays and fades.)

END OF PLAY

THIS FRIDAY, JUNE 15

Jennifer Coates

My eye lands on the photo
of you
from the service, lovingly selected by my brother,
your son,
the one where you
sit on a folding chair in a
verdant garden looking up from your novel, a soft smile,
the fuchsia blouse you wear saying everything
about your lively presence still here
with us. I see your face this morning which starts
like any other,
a Friday work day, dogs fed, child off to school.
but today I ache to write to you, to touch you somehow, you whom
I see and walk with inside me
and yet, no longer
are you out there in
that third person kind of way,
across wine glasses or coffee on a table,
at the other end
of a phone, so I can talk to you about my marriage, people we know,
my sadness and
hopes.

I wonder if the irrepressible sunlight on grass still holding rain from
last night
is the reason, or that my birthday just passed, or
— I feel a thud in my belly as if kicked, a heaviness of heart
that tells me why,
but I must check the package of family memorabilia
my brother just sent
with my original birth certificate
and the papers carrying your obituary.
the date is June 15, today,
9 years ago.
I never forget the
date, but this morning I did,

perhaps that
I could remember anew,
and live the sudden
loss again.

Connections of Hope

Rachel Greenberg

March 23, 2013 started out like any other day. I left my house to do errands like I'd done so many Saturdays before that, but while I was away, my husband Glenn suffered a massive brain hemorrhage.

We never spoke to each other again.

He was rushed to UCLA Ronald Reagan Medical Center where I was immediately told there was no hope. "He's got a brain bleed," the head trauma physician said, "as bad as they come. We'll try and operate, but he's already in coma, say your goodbyes."

Glenn survived the surgery. This didn't surprise me because he was a strong man. He'd gone surfing just that very morning. His vitals were good. He was stable, but he also wasn't waking up from the coma, which was not good at all.

After four days in the ICU Glenn was strong enough to undergo an MRI where we received more bad news. The hemorrhage had caused 80-90% damage in his brain stem. Your brain stem controls your bodily functions, like breathing. There was no coming back from this, so I called his family in New York and gave them the terrible news. We'd keep him on ventilator support until they could come out and say goodbye. Then we would let him go.

I never met anyone like Glenn before. He loved me from the start and never got tired of the chase. He actually went to the same coffee shop every day for three years trying to meet me. It wasn't until a vacation with a close friend in the summer of 1999, where she encouraged me to make a list of eligible men that I thought of Glenn. The mystery man who had been watching me at the local coffee shop back home. I decided then that I'd like to meet this guy and would go looking for him when I got back home.

My first day back, I went to that local coffee shop and there he was, just like so many times before but this time he asked me out. He just blurted it out. "Hi, my name is Glenn. How was your trip to Europe? I heard you were away so I told myself that when I saw you next that I would ask you out. Let's go do something."

That was how we began and we saw or spoke to each other every day after that for the rest of his life.

After Glenn's sudden passing I was immediately thrown into this thing called "GRIEF," without a clue of what to do.

I thought something good would happen, you know, to even out the bad, but quickly learned that things don't work that way. Instead, life just keeps moving forward. I tried everything to help with my grief and nothing worked.

I also felt like I'd became an immediate ghost, an invisible person. I'll never forget the first day back at work after Glenn died. I was walking past a friendly face at the office and assumed he'd come running over to talk about my loss and reassure me that everything was going to be okay.

Instead, he abruptly turned around and walked the other way as if I was the grim reaper coming to get him!

I had really thought that others would come running to my side with never-ending support.

Instead, I was left on my own, so I started searching for answers. I wanted to find out what happens when we die. Where do our loved ones go? Do they watch over us? Can we connect with them? Do they live on in some way?

Just a few nights before Glenn's sudden passing we were having one of our late night conversations in bed when I jokingly said, "What would you do if when you die you wake up and you're in line on a cloud waiting for your robe and harp?" Instead of laughing, he grabbed my hand, looked me right in the eyes and said, "You will be okay."

There were other coincidences too. A lot, actually. Looking back, this gave me drive to find out what this was all about. So I started researching the afterlife. At the same time, I started writing about loss and would share my story wherever and whenever I could. Hearing about others who had also experienced devastating loss gave me the most comfort. I knew I wasn't alone, so I wanted others in my shoes to know this. To give them hope.

Before I knew it I was an invited guest speaker at hospitals, city council meetings and spoke often at UCLA, where Glenn's life ended. The more I talked about my grief, the stronger I became, empowered in a sense. I also felt Glenn's ever loving presence beside me every step of the way.

I've spent the last five years in deep research on all topics death, dying and survival for those left behind and those on the other side. My research has shown that there are two things that help most with grief. #1 is time, and #2 is having an ongoing relationship with your loved one/s who have passed (whatever this means for you). I've learned that having this relationship with our loved ones on the other side brings the most comfort to the bereaved.

In 2017 I launched my foundation, Connections of Hope, where I help others just like me who have experienced the devastating loss of a loved one. I've met thousands of people who never want to forget their loved ones who has passed.

I've learned that love never dies. We never have to let go of our love for our loved ones on the other side. There can be hope after loss.

Glenn lived a purposeful life. I am living that purposeful life now and Connections of Hope is that purpose.

I SHALL EVER HOPE

Sara Glerum

The light will be as
dazzling and beautiful as
a Cascades' sunrise.

A silent morning scarlet sky.
A silent teardrop-wake.
A crimson River Styx

flowing inside mourning hearts.
I and the others still
will be in the night,
and you—my love—
will be in the
morning light.

Then the mourning light
will be diffused
and the sadness
will be shuttered
and the razzle-dazzle sunlight
will be blinding.

I, now far behind you,
will feel sorrow,
missing you, and envious
of those who greet you now.
And I shall ever hope for
me, too. I shall ever hope.

THE STORY OF ALL WAS LOVE

Kristina Ashley

There are experiences in life that end up taking us places that we could have never imagined for ourselves. This creation of my book, *All Was Love*, has become a journey that has taken me on paths that could not have happened otherwise. It all began over twenty years ago, on a warm fall day in rural Michigan. If you have read *All was Love*, this story will make it even more meaningful to you. If you have not, what I share with you, I hope at the very least, will open your heart to embracing more of life's miracles and LOVE.

September 16, 1996, I was living on a beautiful farm in Michigan that my boyfriend at the time, owned. Over 200 acres of rolling hills, woods, a river and quality farmland. It was a very powerful time in my life, full of great personal and spiritual awakening. I meditated and journaled daily. I was wide open to what the Universe presented to me on many levels.

I stood in the kitchen of the very old farmhouse, watching out the window as leaves were turning to soft amber colors. Squirrels were running fanatically across the yard, gathering nuts. Life felt lovely in each moment until in an instant, everything seemed to jump to another reality.

My boyfriend came over to me with tears in his eyes from a phone call he had received. He had been informed that his eighteen-year-old cousin, Tammy, that had just graduated high school that year, had not survived an accident, and had died. I found myself in shock that something like that could happen so close to someone I cared about deeply. I had never met Tammy personally, but I knew that everyone in my boyfriend's family adored her.

The tragic account of three young cousins having a good time, not really thinking things through, drinking, driving and rolling a jeep over on a sharp curve, spilled from his lips wet with tears that were full of shock and grief. The story went on about how an older cousin was driving the jeep that Tammy's brother owned. Somehow the brother and cousin had survived the bad accident. The families of both children were not only distraught from the loss of Tammy, but Tammy's parents were very angry at the older cousin for driving when he had been drinking. Now the two families were enraged and at odds while dealing with this tragedy.

After comforting my boyfriend with hugs and kind expressions, I found myself having a strong desire to go outside and sit in the sun. I had always called the farm that we lived on, "Heaven's Gate." It was an almost surreal looking place with so many different kinds of stunning flowers, big old trees, and peaceful spots to just look out at the world from and be contemplative. As I sat down on the back porch, I wondered what memories Tammy had had there. My boyfriend had bought the farm from his grandparents, which were also her grandparents. I was just sitting there on the back porch steps, quietly, so quietly, and that is when I felt her.

My face was bathing in the sun. The air felt full of life somehow. Something was moving. All around me there was so much good energy. I felt heightened in my senses, open and peaceful. It was in this peace that I felt her fully. I have no idea how I know this, but to this day so many years later, I know this clearly, like I know my very own name. She was just energy. Light and high. She was in the trees and on the ground and part of the flowers. Somehow she spoke to me, in energy, not words, but I understood exactly what she was saying, and why. I didn't really understand her with my mind. I understood her with all of my being. Every cell of me absorbed her communication in a way that overwhelmed me and I began to weep. My physical, emotional and spiritual hearts just blew right open and in a miraculous instant, I understood about life and death and love and God.

Her energy kept moving around and through me and I knew that as a writer I had to try to put onto paper what I was understanding. It was hard to stand up, as I felt like I was in a dream.

Everything felt fluid somehow. I don't consciously remember getting a pen and paper from inside the house, I just remember knowing that I needed them and then having them in my hands. I walked back outside, sat down and an interpretation of what Tammy was experiencing flowed out of me as a poem. It came to me from this place that Tammy was in. The place of pure consciousness. Not only did the poem "All Was Love" come, but the understanding of the big picture and what was important to her was clear to me.

She wanted her family not to fight about or be in despair over the loss of her, but to let their hearts be full and forgiving. Because in the big scheme of things, LOVE is all there is and God is LOVE and there is no need to waste any moment's thought on anything less. In effect, she expressed what the "dying" experience was like and there was nothing to fear. That when you die, you just transition out of your body, back into the consciousness of being one with everything. I was in awe because not only was I understanding her, it felt as if my whole being was experiencing what she was experiencing...I was one with everything and in those moments, knew nothing but LOVE.

When I felt more back into my body, I went back into the house and read the poem to my boyfriend and he cried. He was not a person who was very comfortable with emotions so we didn't speak much about it. A few weeks later he told me that the older cousin, Robert, who had been driving the while intoxicated, as well as Tammy's brother Randy, may have to go to jail for their part in the negligence that caused her death. A warrant had been issued for her brother Randy because he was the owner of the vehicle, and let his cousin Robert drive it while intoxicated. Instantly, I felt such compassion for the two cousins and I was completely aware that Tammy did not want them to suffer. Not the suffering from a court case or possible jail time or the current inner suffering they were experiencing. I felt intensely compelled to write to the court on her behalf and try to state things in a way that would help them. I wrote that letter and I don't know if it helped, but I do know that Randy didn't go to prison. I do not know what happened with Robert.

The story goes on and on, right up to this very moment. My experience with Tammy, when her soul made its transition, truly helped shape my life. I became a Hospice volunteer, as I no longer had any fear of death, and I wanted to help others go through their "dying" experience in a peaceful way. I became a better mother, knowing that if I just focused on LOVE, my son would have everything he needed. Even as a single parent, I could raise him to be a good man in the world. I started a bachelor's degree with Death and Dying as my minor and Human Services as my major. I became a better writer with a special ability to write about people's lives in a way that moved and inspired others.

Then one day it came to me that I could turn the poem into a gift book that could help those suffering from the loss of a loved one or in the dying process themselves...and this is what I, along with Trea Christopher Grey the Artist, and Kimall Christensen the Graphic Designer have done. I have held onto this experience with Tammy until I could find the perfect kindred spirits to contribute the artwork and book design in a way that would invite people from any walk of life to embrace the words and to know that there is no death.

There is only transition. That each soul has a beautifully transformative experience, and none of them want us to have even one moment of concern. That everything in life is LOVE, and if you can live your life from that knowing now, instead of just realizing it when you die, your whole life can change. It can be a joyful life that makes a difference and a life truly worth living. A life that any soul could be content to leave behind.

THE ART OF LONGING

Dr. Robert A. Niemeyer

This poem arose from a conjunction of events—the recent death of my mother-in-law, the last surviving parent on either side of our family, and my driving for hours through a deep Canadian winter to offer a grief workshop in Brockville. The periodic bursts of long "O" sounds echoed for me the howling wind, and the endlessly receding landscape evoked the landscape of memory and our yearning for return. The sensory pull between the strong draw of the past and my forward momentum found expression in the evolving imagery, and hinted at an essential tension in grieving.

Those of us who have driven
the long cold road alone
have watched the thin line
of trees, frosted white,
slipping behind

like memories.
We know the pull
of something unseen
beyond the reach of dry eyes,
fixed, blinking

at the distant mist.
We ride the road
with our lonely ghosts,
unwavering in their devotion
like penitents at the altar

of our grief.
This is how we perfect
the art of longing,
learn to nurse the hurt,
refuse the fullness

Originally printed in The Art of Longing: Selected Poems by Robert Neimeyer 2009

of this world.
For now, we keep driving,
lean into the dimming light,
lean further toward
winter's receding horizon,

and away from arrival.

THE GREATEST GIZMO

Gwen Goodkin

A few years ago, my mother handed me a set of faded papers browned at the edges and neatly tri-folded to fit in a slim enve-lope. On the first typewritten page was a title, "The Greatest Gizmo," and, underneath, my dad's name and the address of the house he grew up in.

"I thought you might like to have this," she said.

It was a conciliatory gesture, we both knew, since she'd spent much time and energy campaigning for me to give up on writing already and get a real job.

I read the story, which was about a device that could create anything its owner dreamed up—a spaceship, a mythical beast, an enchanted island. The story was structured like a riddle for the reader to solve—what exactly the "greatest gizmo" was—and, don't fret, the solution would come at the end. I reached the bottom of the last page, which stopped mid-sentence and did not solve the riddle. I went to my mom and said, "But the ending's missing." To which she replied, "I know." She lifted her hands in disappointment.

Doctors told my mom they got all the cancer out of my dad. "They said they might have left a few cells, but everything else was gone," she told me. "Well." She picked at a piece of lint on her shirt. "A few cells are all it takes."

Spinal cancer paralyzed my dad a little at a time, from the feet up. My dad continued to work for as long as his body would allow. He worked in downtown Cleveland's version of the Empire State Building, the Terminal Tower. My mom drove him in the mornings and I rode along. The drive was about an hour-and-a-half round trip, a long time for a kid, but I didn't care. I loved being in the city. It was a world of its own. Entering the streets lined with tall buildings was like being taken in to a huge embrace. I lay down in the backseat so I could see how each building challenged the sky. The city beat with the energy of life. And I loved that my dad was part of it.

On my dad's final trip home from the hospital, paramedics brought him into our house on a stretcher. At that point, he could only move his head. I was in second grade.

In my first-grade school picture, my hair is combed and carefully braided. I'm wearing a dress, country blue with white flowers and a flare of ruffle at the shoulder. I've even snuck a flash of tongue in the side of my smile. In my second grade picture, my hair is messy. I smile with my mouth, but not my eyes. I'm wearing a jumper whose straps hang crooked.

Not long after that picture was taken, I woke earlier than usual, before dawn, and opened my bedroom door. Every light was on. I made a slow trail to our family room, pushed my back against a wall and watched my dad die. Then, just like it was any other school day, I returned to my room, changed into my Catholic school uniform and boarded the bus. At school, about four kids stood in line in front of the teacher, waiting to talk to her. I joined them.

"Guess what?" said each kid.

"What?" said my teacher. She was enjoying the game. One kid told her his TV had been knocked out by lightning.

"Guess what?" I said.

"What?"

"My dad died."

Her face went slack. I hadn't cried all morning. I'd stuffed all that in the pit of my ribs. But, when I saw my teacher's face, all the stuffing came out. I tried to push everything back inside, but it was too strong.

The principal came for me. I didn't like the principal. None of us kids did. We speculated she stopped being a nun when the schools did away with beatings.

"Can I see Miss Jack?" I asked. Miss Jack had been my first grade teacher. I liked her and she liked me, even though I'd shouted "Done!" once after a test to prove not only was I the smartest, but the fastest, too. Miss Jack took away all my tickets for that. Every week we got five tickets and, if we did something bad, we had a ticket taken away. At the end of the week we could buy stuff with our tickets. The kids with all their tickets got the best stuff. I didn't care so much about puppy stickers or rainbow erasers, but I did care about keeping all my tickets. The tickets proved I was good. And, if I was good, God would make my dad better.

Over the years, we've found bits and pieces of my dad's writing. "The Greatest Gizmo."

Dungeons and Dragons™ storylines from games with my brother. A chunk of a typewritten science fiction novel. The beginning of another, handwritten science fiction novel. But never a complete story or manuscript.

I didn't know about his writing when he was alive. As far as I was concerned, my dad's hobby was music. He played Beatles music on an organ that stood near the front door of our house. He played the saxophone in high school and when it was time for me to join the school band, I was handed his clarinet. Maybe because I didn't get to choose my instrument, but more likely because my dad wasn't around to teach me or push me to do better, I never really took to music. What my dad and I did share, though, was a true love of stories. He read to me every day, especially when he became confined to a bed. And later, I read to him.

My mom and I never did find the ending of "The Greatest Gizmo," which seems fitting and like my dad's own story: one that ended too soon. My best guess at the riddle's solution—the magical device that created whatever its owner dreamed up?

A typewriter.

STANDING IN THE GAP

Toni Lepeska

He called me "doll." He took me to see the Empire State Building when I was 16. He introduced me to art at the Peabody Museum at Yale University. Years later, I was all grown up, and he was lying in a hospital bed. He told me I was like a daughter to him.

I was his niece. He was my last surviving uncle.

I wailed when I learned he'd died. It wasn't only that he was dead. I'd missed seeing him once more. Missed helping him into eternity. Missed saying goodbye.

He lived to be 85. In a society uncomfortable with expressions of grief, we overlook the impact of the death of uncles and aunts. They sit lower on the hierarchy of loss. They don't typically live with us. They aren't in that tight family circle. Not a spouse. Not a child. Not a sibling. Not a parent. But like a parent. After we lose our mothers and fathers, they stand in the gap, that void created as our elders die. They know all the good stories about our parents. And the stories about our early childhoods. They knew us in diapers.

Uncle Karl was my father's only brother and eight years his senior, but they looked so much alike their relationship was unmistakable. The same dark hair. The same glasses. The same heads that required oversized hats. My uncle stood a few inches taller than my six-foot-tall Dad.

He towered above me. A New Englander, my uncle had a distinguished way of holding his mouth, accentuated by his mustache. Strangers often mistook him for a college professor. In fact, he loved learning and took college courses in philosophy and art well into the second half of his life.

I was a teenager when I visited my uncle's Connecticut home for the first time. His car broke down and then broke down again. I was turned out into the crush of people at LaGuardia Airport, a Mississippi girl alone in what was then the second most populous city in the world. I called my parents and found a seat. Within the hour, I spotted Uncle Karl. His head, turning one way and then another, bobbed above the crowd. He was afraid he'd lost his brother's daughter.

Over the years, I wrote frequently to my uncle and aunt and visited several times, but after illness struck our home, I didn't see

Connecticut again for 12 years. In 2010, I returned with my husband in tow. It was the year after my mother died, and four years after my father's death.

My plane landed after dark, and I met my uncle in the parking lot of a Marriott. The lights of our rental car hit his, revealing the distinctive outline of my uncle's head. I gasped.

"He looks just like dad," I said.

I nearly cried.

After the reunion, I visited almost every year. My uncle was always the perfect host, but I realized after he took my husband and me to the Beardsley Zoo in Bridgeport, sat on a bench and told us to go enjoy ourselves, that my uncle wasn't the same. Over the years, we'd walked miles together exploring Connecticut. Now he couldn't make it much farther than the zoo gate.

The year I didn't visit, he fell on the steps of his home and broke his leg in three places.

Nothing was the same for my uncle after that. He was a back and forth resident of a rehabilitation hospital. I visited twice that year, and called and wrote frequently.

His neighbor, Anita, a distant relative, called me to his side one spring day, the 10th year after my dad's death. I bought a plane ticket that afternoon, and the next morning set out from Memphis. Anita met me at the New Haven airport at 10 that night. We packed the luggage into the back, and I climbed into the passenger seat of her SUV. And then Anita's smile dissolved.

"Karl didn't make it," she said.

A cascade of pain, anger and disappointment erupted from my mouth.

"No! No!" I collapsed my head into my hands. "No!"

My uncle had died the night before in his bed.

The passing street lights looked like starbursts through my tears as we made the 20-minute drive to Milford, where the Lepeska brothers had grown up. I had called it my second home, but that night I wanted to run away. My daddy wasn't there, and my uncle wasn't there. I wanted to crawl into a hole and mourn.

My aunt met me at her door. We embraced. Childless, she was alone now. I helped plan the graveside service, held several days later. I sang the chorus of a hymn, "Because He Lives."

A paid church soloist at one time, my uncle loved music. He had piano in his office. We had to have music.

Uncle Karl had mailed a letter to me the year of our reunion. I'd left my longtime job as a newspaper reporter, jumped from a cliff, so of speak, to work for myself. To be a freelance writer. A new wife, too, I felt as though I was embarking on an exciting but uncertain adventure.

Out of the blue, Uncle Karl's one-page letter arrived.

"You have made a wonderful decision ... (that) has taken a lot of courage," he wrote.

"No matter how it develops, it will be worth it – well worth the effort. This is something I truly believe."

A few months before he died, I wrote to him and told him the letter is "now and will forever be an encouragement to me."

I keep my uncle's letter on my desk. I will always keep it on my desk.

My uncle stood in the gap. Now he is gone, but his indelible mark on my life will never die.

I'm the grownup now, and it's my turn to stand in the gap.

AN ASSHOLE IN PLAIN VIEW

Paul Boardman

"Love makes your soul crawl out from its hiding place."
ZORA NEALE HURSTON

I met the family—Susan his wife; Caitlyn and Lisa, his daughters—right after they viewed and identified their man, Paul (66), a veteran. Paul had checked into the hospital with flu-like symptoms and then discovered he had pancreatic cancer. It was all very sudden. They thought Paul would survive this battle, too. But then he suddenly got worse and died. The family was shaken up and tearful. In shock. When the nurse asked them which funeral home they wanted, Lisa named ours, the only one she knew, because she drove by it every day. Now death was more than a passing glance through the windshield. In 48 hours, I'd host Paul's memorial.

After we shook hands, Lisa said, smiling through tears, "I guess it's fitting that you're a Paul, too."

I would learn that Paul joined the Army in 1967. While battling in Vietnam, he was exposed to Agent Orange, the defoliant used by the Americans to strip the jungles so they could see their enemies. In the 1990s, Paul was given full medical discharge benefits. His symptoms progressively worsened.

We sat down, and I offered a sample Order of Service and described the elements, any of which they could change. They said they didn't plan to write an obituary until after the memorial. And I said, okay, but the story of that person's life grounds the leave-taking. It's important to review what he did, where he walked, how he spent his time, what his primary concerns were, who he was connected to, who he was born to and who he leaves behind; to reflect, in a plain-spoken manner, on the span of his life. The anecdotes, vignettes and storytelling are the meat on this frame.

"So, tell me about Paul," I said. "What would you say about him to help me know him?"

"Well, the first thing," Caitlyn blurted out, "is that he was an asshole!"

All three of them laughed, so I laughed along, a little uncomfortably. The assholes I'd known were no laughing matter. But they cried and laughed.

"Yeah, he was the crankiest son of a bitch. So damn cranky," Lisa announced. They laughed harder.

Susan, the wife, piled on, "He was a prickly scorpion. Stubborn as an ass."

They cackled while they cried.

I felt at ease then. This grouchiness was his identity: he was the lovable crank, a lovely curmudgeon. They could say these things because they adored him. The caricature of him as lovable asshole warmed them.

"He was a tender-hearted marshmallow, a teddy bear. He loved nothing more than to spoil his wife and his girls. The Grouch Syndrome was just his way of loving you on his terms. That way he didn't have to expend his energy on people he didn't like. He would just push them away. If he liked you, he teased you. If he didn't like you, he provoked you," Lisa said.

Caitlyn declared, "He was my hero. I aspire to be him. He never did anything to make people like him. He cared the least for people's approval of anyone I've ever known."

The picture of Paul didn't totally come into focus; I couldn't understand how such a man, such a "character" could really be a role model, though authenticity sounded about right. Being true to himself. Still, I was fuzzy on how to admire him. I chose to just take them at their word. Their responsiveness to him was so overwhelmingly positive.

Two days later, I praised a man who didn't just tolerate but embraced the consequence of wholly being himself. Paul stood uncamouflaged before his people, a bare trunk in clear view.

In the hospital, Paul said, "After I'm gone, cry for 15 minutes. Then, have a party. Celebrate how much I loved you."

Paul had scrabbled his way through the jungle. This was a war he had won.

Originally printed in Gravel *magazine produced by the MFA Program in Creative Writing, University of Arkansas at Monticello*

THE MEMORIAL

Toti O'Brien

They held a memorial for her, grand and unconventional—a large show devoted to the art form she had loved and promoted. A myriad of artists who had known her were asked to create a piece. All must have accepted...

The show was a triumph, the crowd dense, impressive. Having contributed, I was there. As I tried to look at the art, its quantity soon overwhelmed me. And all I could see, anyway, were fragments, cutouts framed by people's heads, torsos, limbs. Or jackets, coats, backpacks. Though I had come a long distance, I felt I should give up.

Instead I persevered. I needed to see my tribute. I had a hard time recognizing it. On my studio walls it had seemed evocative of her, of our friendship. Not here. Now it looked like a shell on a shore, after the tide vomits whatever the bottom hid. A star in the sky, when you try to find constellations and you can't—a blurred, shifting dot in a blinding multitude. A word in a language unknown, indecipherable.

What did I expect? Identities are lost in a crowd. Is meaning as well? So I felt, perhaps because my piece originally had meant a whole lot. It was generated by meaning—by a need to remember my friend and our deep connection. Send one last farewell.

I missed air. I headed out, glimpsing at people I knew and should acknowledge. Not an easy task. They appeared and vanished, submerged by the crowd. To elbow my way amidst the human maze didn't seem advisable. Accordingly with protocol, they were also talking nonstop, and I didn't wish to interrupt them. I preferred to catch their gaze at a distance, smile waving my hand. 'Oh,' their eyes seemed to tell when they met mine, 'you're here! I'll see you in a moment.' They'd promptly forget.

At openings I feel my acquaintances have rarely time to devote me. Why is that? I have nothing to give career wise. I don't trade in opportunities. I'm not even an ego flatterer—I pay a few compliments, matter of fact, when I have fresh and genuine ones. Therefore I'm a kind of odd ball, not a total misfit but almost. And she was the same.

The woman we were celebrating would have found it demanding, I know, to stroll amidst this crazy rumpus. She wouldn't have lasted, though art was her absolute passion. But in single doses, like for me.

On these very guidelines we understood each other in a private way, un-belonging to such formal gathering. Again my chest tightened.

I extracted myself from the cobweb and I stepped outside. I'd wait for a while, then plunge in once more, wave to someone else. But my feet proceeded to the lot where my car was parked.

I met him at the entrance. He stopped, stared at me, then he smiled. We stood, looking at one another. We greeted then, vivaciously, warmly. He was headed to the memorial I had just left. I didn't tell, obviously, how briefly I had lasted.

Her memory grasped me as I saw him. As much as the tributes affixed on the walls had drowned grief with senseless repeating, his features made her come alive.

I had met him on the day she died. In fact two hours earlier. I had just showed up without calling, inspired by an irrational feeling. I knew she was sick, and how much. I had visited before but with notice. That day I drove without previous planning.

She would die, but we didn't know how long the process would take. As soon as I entered I did. It would take no time. She was clearly unconscious, but those who surrounded her hadn't realized it. Two relatives were at her side—a close kin, quite young, another one come from abroad. This last an old man, calm and grounded, whereas the young fellow was anguished, worn. They had been up for hours. Fatigue blurred their vision, and of course proximity. A pair of fresh eyes, an outsider, were certainly needed.

I noticed her agony had started. I hadn't yet done it—tell folks their beloved has stepped into no return zone. I had seen the zone previously, at least—believe me, then you cannot miss it. It has its own aura, its own unmistakable profile.

I told them. The young man's response sounded panicky, but it was despair. He sought help and found some by phone. We took turns performing the comforting gestures that can't cure, but can alleviate. I was glad of being included since I wasn't family... at those times a line is usually drawn. And they could have done it, but didn't.

I was very grateful. An immigrant, I lacked blood connections on site. I had formed new ones based on affinity. She was one of my strongest ties. In fact she was family, and more. But how could I expect my unorthodox concept to be understood? In such situation?

The old man did. The young one was with her, exclusively. He listened to her heartbeat, he focused on her pulse that first grew irregular, frantic, then finally weakened. The old man embraced a wider horizon. His age might have provided perspective. In spite of his pain he allowed my presence. By letting me help he created a whole, a togetherness where the four of us belonged.

Yes, the four of us shared the ritual in the unifying presence of that weird thing, spreading. That thing invading the room, exuded by the walls, rising from the floor, suspended by the ceiling. So enormous it blotted us away. Of course it was death, but I could say life. They couldn't be parted. We couldn't, we wouldn't attempt such a split. It was death and life, love as well—the unexpected output of their instantaneous collision.

Oh yes, it was love. I can reconstruct every instant of that afternoon. I'd rather not to, but I can. Somehow it was preserved intact. Whatever was there feels like love, though I am prudent while using such term. It rarely applies. But it snapped at me like a rubber band, briskly released—there, on the concrete of the parking lot, when I saw the old man.

I didn't know his name, he didn't know mine. No idea where he lived, where he flew from, where he would return. Did I care? What for? Shall we attend other agonies, because we had managed so well? Of course not. I would never see him again, as I wouldn't see my dead friend.

Still there it was, love. It snapped in my face when we greeted. I suspect he was hit as well. He must have been swept, as I was, by the breath of something we can't either own or control. It shows up when it so decides, a fragile impression, unsigned.

SILENCE ACROSS THE SIDEYARDS | FOR DIANE

Mary Langer Thompson

The eve of your daughter's wedding
I am drawn toward home.
I park in front
of where we used to live.
Two houses,
side by side,
repeopled, remodeled,
remembered.

Fresh from Chicago
we moved in.
California, 1956.
Dad cleaned and scrubbed,
unable to find work.
Mom took a job at Citizen's Bank

Tired of Our Miss Brooks
and Mr. Ed's peanut buttered palate,
I wandered outside
dissolving a grape fizzy on my tongue.
There you were,
ten years old with blonde braids.
Of course your eyes were blue,
and we hula-hooped
from strangers to sidekicks.

You taught me to polka
down your hallway,
past your room
directly across from mine.
Soon I started to whistle
across the sideyards
whenever I had news.
You would appear,

see me
curlered and Clearasiled.

After school we'd dance
to American Bandstand.
Overnight, we'd ride Route 66
to see Steve Allen.
You learned to drive first.
Of course your car was blue.

A whistle
and soon a light
to share moments from dates,
while your dog, Lucky,
paced beneath our windows.

Between learning and teaching
we married.
I stood in your wedding--
(of course my dress was blue)
and you in mine.
We birthed our babies
a month apart.
Yours will marry tomorrow.

The disease
bombarded your blood
and took you quickly.
Within three days.
We buried you in blue.

A woman now collects
autumn leaves,
and rose petals,
like tears,
lie on the lawn.
I strain to hear
a whisper of a whistle,
but all I hear is
silence across the sideyards.

LULLABY

Will Silverman

Someone sing me a lullaby
Let me cry for a moment
Let me run to your arms now
Fold into your magic

There were dreams
Wrapped in blankets
There was light in shadows
Where'd it all go, all go?

Through time, I'd forgotten
When my lungs opened fully
And each breath meant tomorrow
Would deliver vivid dawn

Now, I walk alone and wonder
When life turned
Fire burned coal to ash
And a spark no longer lived inside

Lingering lies limit vision
To a past unknown
The depth of my soul
Trapped and hungry, leads me

Once again, I strive
To ride wind
To follow raindrops
Through clouds and sorrow
Driving seeds from arid ground

Whistle Down the Wind

Beth Rahe Balas

Certain events in life turn you inside out, spin you 'round, and spit you out reborn. As a tender 18-year-old from the suburbs, going to a rugged college campus my freshman year totally altered my life. It was a time where I discovered adventure, the outdoors, and, um... men.

The tiny town of Mont Alto straddles Pennsylvania and Maryland, just east of West Virginia, near the Mason Dixon Line. When Penn State's main campus is full, freshmen select from a menu of satellite campuses. The girl in front of me in my high school homeroom was headed there. I'd only recently moved to Pennsylvania from Illinois, so I accepted her offer to room together at Mont Alto with a shrug. I had no idea that the campus historically educated foresters and surveyors (my major was Visual Art), nor that the ratio of men to women was 8:1. (Nor that my future roommate was a practicing wiccan, but that's another tale.)

Nestled in the Appalachian mountains, I discovered hiking, camping, climbing, rappelling, and spelunking, finding challenge and new friends. It was vastly different than either of my high schools, especially St.Louise de Marillac Academy for Girls. Late night conversations found me re-evaluating everything I'd known before.

Robert Jeffrey Hawk lived downstairs in Mrs. Duffield's boarding house and became a favorite partner-in-philosophy. Lanky, with a wicked sense of humor, he had robin's egg blue eyes, a wry grin, and some very unfamiliar (to me) personal dogma. He admired hard physical labor, and incongruously, the shaman Carlos Castaneda. Hawk eschewed popular music, preferring to whistle along with classic cowboy blues.

Sophomore year, we both transitioned to main campus. After late nights sessions in my art studio, I'd meet Hawk outside the all-night Campus Diner at the edge of campus. We'd talk so intensely that we'd just sit down on the curb in rapt conversation. Then we'd head inside for grilled sticky buns, and after more talk, race to my apartment, as young lovers do. We did, anyway.

The next year, we each lived in far flung rentals way outside of town, in opposite directions.

Hawk wanted more. He was offered forested property with a creek and lots of fir trees to build an authentic log cabin, which we did together with friends. It had no plumbing, so he'd often come over to my house for showers.

He'd promised to come over one Saturday night for dinner, after going for a run. Around 10 o'clock, I began to wonder where he was. The farmhouse kitchen phone rang; it was our friend Dan. It was so late that I reflexively said, "What's up? Who died?" Dan paused and told me that when Hawk had gone out for a run, he'd been hit by a drunk driver (probably from the football game) who had fled the scene. Hawk had been airlifted to a hospital on the other side of the mountains. I don't know how I got there, but I followed immediately.

When his parents denied me permission to visit his room in order to "remember him as he was," my imagination took me on a wild ride, fearing he'd been gruesomely mangled. I walked the halls until I found him, and peered through the open door. I was relieved to see him lying intact, though ashen and comatose, and hooked up to blinking and whirring machines.

Hawk died a few nights later, while I slept on a friend's floor at a nearby college. Inexplicably, the sound of him whistling close by my ear woke me precisely at 4:35 a.m, which I later learned was the exact time that he died. When Hawk's family tasked me with calling to inform our friends, I learned I wasn't the only one who awoke to this farewell whistle from the other side.

Later that day, his kind father put his arm around my shoulder. As we looked out the hospital window at the mountains together, he offered me some words of wisdom. First, to allow at least a year to catch my breath, and while "you never forget, it gets easier after that." Secondly, that some people are like brilliant October leaves, a burst of intensity, and then - they're gone.

I was 19, Hawk was only 20. He was just the first of many that would fall in quick succession. A few days after Hawk died, my roommate's sister was killed in a car crash on black ice. A close friend's mother died suddenly that month. Heck, my horse Buck even developed a case of fatal stomach torsion. On the "bright" side, a nasty redneck who had raped me and several other women our freshman year, died (so there) of his own stupidity by driving without headlights, on, and then off, a mountain road on a moonless night.

Then there was Jack, also from Mont Alto campus, a housemate from that communal farmhouse at Penn State. A few years later, he travelled to see me before my wedding to persuade me unsuccessfully) to marry him instead. A great dancer and musician, he was so intent on his dream to own a farm that he worked for years as a truck driver to buy his land. He got his farm but died from testicular cancer shortly afterwards. And there were more: my friend John's 41-year-old father died from a rare virus that attacked his heart, next, John's twin brother from leukemia. Their uncle that lived with them died of a heart attack shortly thereafter.

This "death vortex" deeply shocked and shaped me for some time, though fortunately, it turned out to be unique. I rebounded by quickly marrying a man whose life had also been shaped by loss and family tragedy. In time, I learned that healing is a choice, and an individual path.

I've had miscarriages, lost other friends, and both my parents since then. Each loss brings up all of the others. Losing all those friends so long ago is a very fundamental part of who I am. I don't understand why there was so much tragedy in such a short time; life certainly is unpredictable.

I try to remember that. I never... EVER... want life to think it has to teach me that lesson again.

Attachments

Donna James

I see his body
I cannot   feel
him   anywhere

like a breeze lifting
gone

pale yellow moth dead   on the sill
seed of a sunflower
on the path   from sofa to door
shreds
I gather   his parting gifts

THE RING

Diana Burbano

This play is dedicated to Gabriel Zimmerman

ANDIE Small and delicate looking, 28 F strong willed.

MR. ROSS Proprietor of a consignment 65 M jewelry shop.

A small Arizona consignment shop.

7 minutes

Carefree AZ. A pretty little consignment jewelry shop. Andie, 30, stands uncertainly, waiting.

Mr.Ross enters.

MR. ROSS Hello there!

ANDIE Yes. I buzzed—

MR. ROSS Of course. Sorry it took so long. I'm a one man operation!

ANDIE I'd like to, uh, sell this. (She takes off an engagement ring) It's, um, a size 5—

MR. ROSS It's quite beautiful. Do you want to sit?

ANDIE I'm OK.
She is teary.

MR. ROSS Do you want a cup of tea?

ANDIE No. I just want to drop off the ring.

MR. ROSS Of course. Let's fill out the papers.

ANDIE I don't need papers.

MR. ROSS Miss, this is a valuable piece of jewelry.

ANDIE It's really OK.

MR. ROSS I can't take it without filling out the consignment paperwork

ANDIE Maybe 1 should give it to Goodwill.

MR. ROSS Miss—

ANDIE Or throw it into the Grand Canyon.

MR. ROSS (Gently) You're not from Carefree..

ANDIE Tucson. I got in the car this morning and just kept going. I needed to see the desert.

MR.ROSS This is a lovely ring.

ANDIE He got it at an estate sale.

MR.ROSS I see.

ANDIE My fiancé died.

MR. ROSS I'm so sorry for your loss.

ANDIE I'm not sure it is my loss. We weren't married yet. I don't really have any say in what the family does with his-- His dad put together a memorial trail run today. He loved to run, in the desert especially. In fact when he gave me this, we were sweaty from being on a 3 hour hike, and I'm drinking water and I turn around and the goofball is kneeling in the Sonoran desert. And I'm like, "What's the matter?" I though he'd tripped, and he was holding this sweet little box, and I couldn't-- I mean I started to laugh, and he started to laugh, and I think we scared off every jackrabbit and coyote for miles around we laughed so hard. I was like, "You couldn't do this when I wasn't sweaty and gross?" But it was perfect, you know? I figured we'd be running trails together for a long time. We'd only been engaged a couple of weeks when he—

MR. ROSS I'm so sorry.

ANDIE I mean, I didn't really get to know his family too well yet. I work a lot, and so, we'd only really had a couple of dinner together. We were just learning to get comfortable with each other. And now, I don't really have any-- place-- in all this. I'm not his wife. I'm not "official" and so, I don't get to participate-- I didn't choose where to put him, and I don't have his name. All I have are some beautiful memories and this ring. And now even the memories feel-- false.

MR. ROSS You should put the ring in a safe place.

ANDIE There is no such thing. I mean, a grocery store, that's supposed to be a safe place right? And that's where he-- He was protecting his boss. He loved working for her, for the people. He was good with constituents.

MR.ROSS Tucson. (It dawns on him)

ANDIE My fiancé was in the back and he stepped in front of a little girl. 9. Really little. They both died.

MR.ROSS I read about it.

ANDIE How do you feel about guns? Do you have one?

MR.ROSS I do.

ANDIE This isn't exactly a high crime area.

MR.ROSS I have a lot of fine goods. I have to be able to protect myself.

ANDIE Have you ever shot anyone?

MR.ROSS I was in Vietnam.

ANDIE Did you enjoy it?

MR.ROSS Miss. Take the ring. Please. Go home.

ANDIE They brought him to my hospital. He was gone before he arrived though. The team worked on the little girl, but she died on the table.

MR.ROSS It looks like the Congresswoman might recover. Brave woman.

ANDIE Yes.

She looks at the ring.

MR.ROSS Do you want me to call someone?

ANDIE No. I want you to take this ring. And when someone walks in here, and is looking for something special, give them this ring so that they can have the life we were supposed to have.

MR.ROSS But—

ANDIE And don't tell them where it came from.

MR.ROSS I'll keep this. Come back, and it will be here for you.

ANDIE You meet a guy, fall in love, you look at wedding chapels and the next day he's --gone. I miss him so much. I miss the wedding we never had, the babies we never held, the trails we never ran. (A beat.) You'll be keeping that ring a long time.

MR.ROSS Nevertheless. It will be here when you're ready.

Andie stops. She looks out the window.

ANDIE It's pretty here.

MR.ROSS Most beautiful little piece of the Sonoran desert you ever saw.

ANDIE Maybe I'll go for a walk.

MR.ROSS Ba careful, it's getting dark.

ANDIE It doesn't matter.

MR.ROSS I like to look up at the stars. You see millions of them.

ANDIE One star for everyone who's been shot. And one for everyone still mourning them.

Andie exits. Mr. Ross takes the ring, puts it in a box and puts the box in a drawer.

BLACKOUT.

The Ring was originally published in the "All Too Short" Collection by Code Red Playwrights, honoring lives cut short by gun violence.

NOT THE MERRY WIDOW

Sara J Glerum

When the mail came today, I sorted through it. The standard junk —brochures for cruises, requests from political causes, a handful of cheesy looking greeting cards to benefit a cause I don't support, department store coupons, and another condolence letter (wow, I hadn't thought of her for years!)—then, at the bottom of the pile, my Opera Magazine. I quickly scanned the articles touted in bold lettering on its cover and burst into tears. Big, inconsolable sobs.

Setting down the pile of mail, I frantically walked into the next room. Turning on my heels and returning, I picked up the magazine and shoved it into a desk drawer. I was trembling and crying, both. I didn't want to see it again or think about what was making me react this way. But I continued to cry, and because I was alone (as I always am now), I could cry as loud as I wanted. So I did.

It took that episode to make me recognize another facet of my new life as a recent widow, another dimension to my bereavement and yet another adjustment to be made. The headline itself was benign: THAT BROADWAY SOUND—HOW VOCALISM IN MUSICAL THEATRE HAS EVOLVED OVER THE DECADES. It was the word "Broadway" that triggered my emotional response. My husband had been a long-standing insider in the workings of backstage Broadway. Because of him, I've met movers and shakers of New York's theatre scene and shaken hands with some of the hottest stars of Broadway. Now that world is closed off to me—like a big street barricade was just erected announcing "No Admittance." It hit me that never again will I travel inside that privileged circle.

Adjusting to the death of a spouse is a huge deal; no one argues that. Thousands of day-to-day events have to be re-thought, re-orchestrated and rehashed. Adjustments are rampant; everywhere I turn, something is missing or needs to be done differently—from the way I do the laundry and set the table, to the size of the table itself and how much coffee I brew every morning.

I have learned where the air intake is for my car, to reset the wireless router, pay bills on a different online setup, and diagnose what's wrong with the furnace thermostat. I, alone, go to the cleaners, fill the gas tank, make oil change appointments, and renew the license tabs. Even the things I used to do happily seem daunting because

'I'm it' forever. Trash hauling, shredder emptying, light bulb changing, clock winding, and smoke-alarm battery changes are all mine.

Many friends have expressed willingness to help with projects requiring ladders and electrical know-how; projects requiring tool savvy and technical expertise. I'm lucky—people are wanting to help me, hoping to make themselves feel better, too, because their friend is gone, while they're still here. Most routine chores don't require assistance—just time, and doing everything absorbs so much of each day, like a giant sponge wiping away leisure time. Why does this simple stuff seem so overwhelming!

To be fair, let me mention that not everything is bad. I have more closet space, and will never need to iron hankies or prepare *runny* scrambled eggs again. I can eat dinner whenever *I'm* hungry and go to bed when I finish my book without a without keeping my husband awake. I'm making my way in a world I've not inhabited for more than fifty years—the world where every decision I make only involves me because I'm single. I can leave cupboard doors open, make eggplant my entire dinner, crank the volume on Bach till the rafters rock, and sleep in the middle of the bed. For a short while those 'me things' lift my grief like a hot air balloon. I am making progress on this long journey of grief.

The *Opera* magazine caused me to confront a piece of my life that I hadn't thought about yet. I loved going backstage with my husband, *especially* in New York, and thoroughly enjoyed accompanying him to conferences for theatrical professionals. I shared in his fame just by standing in his shadow. I'm realizing my identity as his wife clearly meant more to me than I'd realized. No longer will I get the royal backstage tours designed to show off the latest technical expertise to my husband. No more socializing with theatre technicians, listening to their "can you top this" stories of actors botching entrances, dropping lines, or personal fetishes. No longer will technical theatre professionals shake my hand to say thank me for my role encouraging and allowing my husband to . . . write his book, teach his workshops, inspect their theatres. I was thanked just for being "Mrs. Glerum."

Before I became a widow, I would have gone out of my way to prove myself an independent woman, proud of my own accomplishments on my own terms. Now I grasp just how much I enjoyed being associated professionally with my husband, and what a void the absence of that privilege leaves in my identity.

It's hard enough to suffer the loss of my husband without my best and dearest friend—him—to help me through it. I feel as if something akin to a wedge-shaped chunk of myself was cut out of me. I'd been hoping it would grow back with time—imagining it like bread dough rising in the pan. Now I'm imagining another visual—like those photos of people with disfiguring scar tissue covering sites of horrendous injuries—and I realize the void will never fill in. Instead, I will have scar tissue covering it.

Eventually I'll pull out *Opera* and read the article. I'm interested to see what the author has to say about the change in Broadway vocal quality, which I've noticed myself over the past five decades. First, though, the scar tissue has to get a little thicker.

STAGES OF GRIEF

Vanessa Poster

STAGE 7: SCHIZOPHRENIA
I saw his voice.
I smelled his shadow.
My love, he said,
I did not want to leave you.

STAGE 15: WIDOW BRAIN
You know, when you walk into a room
And forget why?
It's like that—except
I know what I've forgotten: me.

STAGE 1: DENIAL
I am on the landing
halfway up, halfway down
the stairs.
I remember eating dinner.
Bob, his snout over the top stair
stares
My husband could be
upstairs at his desk
killing demons in WarCraft
downstairs in his chair
watching Master Chef

STAGE 48: DAMMIT
He was right,
He did do more dishes.

STAGE 23: SELF-MEDICATING AT DENNY'S WITH CARBS
10-inch plate
8-inch pancakes
Butter, syrup
teabag bleeding
onto napkin

STAGE 27: DESPAIR
Joan Didion calls it
the vortex
a vibrating shadow at the horizon edge
connects to a memory of you
I drown.

STAGE 20: JOY
Sitting on the cracked, bulbous, coffee-brown
leather chair he moved in with
Bob asleep with his head on my thigh
His small black body between my legs
You know the rule:
You cannot wake the dog.
I will sit here as long as I can
until I have to pee.

STAGE 100: PSYCHOSIS
I am paying $90 a month
For a dead guy's cell phone.

STAGE 79: PROGRESS
Thinking about thinking about
dating
More than a day without crying
actually liked that movie
walked 10,000 steps
wrote a poem about something
other than my dead husband.

Grief Posts

Linda Yasutake (Mother)
Madi Williamson (Daughter)

MARCH 19, 2017 MADI:

One week... It feels like yesterday. Thoughts from week one: quantitatively, there are more pros than cons. Losing my father, my mentor, my best friend, and the one I always turned to for support, is undoubtedly the saddest experience ever. He wasn't all that just to me. He was a loving father to me and my brother and to any kid who came along and needed a dad. He was a best friend to so many people and he has been remembered as one who always stepped up to help anyone in need, no questions asked. It smashed my heart to pieces to see how much everyone is going to miss him. I don't want to see you hurting like I am.

But the pros... Every smile is a miracle. Every laugh is stronger, each person I have seen is received with gratitude and love. Every morning that I wake up is wrought with anxiety because I have to navigate this world without him, but I am so, so far from having to do this alone.

Grief is funny. We've tried to give a name and stages to such an abstract and personalized concept and try to help everyone the same way when all of us experience it so differently.

The reality is that grief is accepting that you do not own your thoughts for now, and that's ok. It's going to be unpredictable and scary, and every morning you might wake up a completely different person than you were the day before as you learn to adjust to who you are when you've lost so much of yourself so suddenly.

Grief is portrayed as this horrible period where your life is transformed into a numbing black and white and then slowly the color returns but for me, it's like I see the world in a new light. I have been more present in this past week than I have been in a long, long time. I have laughed hysterically as we share stories, cook, play cards, and give hugs. I have taken my time with messages, texts, and conversations. I have been surrounded by so much light and love and I have seen a million reasons to believe that I am going to be ok in the people around me, and in myself.

Not perfect, not the same, never again normal... But ok. I'm learning to be kinder to myself and more accepting of support from those around me which has not been easy but in all honestly I wouldn't be able to survive this without everyone who has come through our doors.

In the first week I didn't have to go long without a shoulder to lean on. There has been food and flowers, hugs and tears... But damn you all blow my mind with your massive hearts. That's the stuff that makes it worth living. He would have loved it.

My dad nurtured a hell of a community, the fact that all of you have been so willing to show up for us is nothing short of awe-inspiring, but it's a testament to the investment that he put into supporting all of us. Obviously I don't wish that such sad circumstances were bringing us together, but thus far I have no regrets about how we've all handled this loss. He was my dad, but he was our Jim.

I don't know what else to say but thank you. From the bottom of my heart.

Extra credit points go to everyone who brought a baby, and to my dearest friend Mohammad who put his insane schedule from CRNA school aside and flew up to spend the weekend making sure his partner in humanitarianism was ok. And she will be, thanks to this big, loud, and unbelievably loving family.

APRIL 3, 2017 LINDA:

Three weeks tonight. Time is a funny thing. These pictures seem like they were taken yesterday (really taken in 1985), but it feels like Jim has been gone for such a long time. I realized the other day that Jim has been part of my daily life since I was 18 years old. That's a lot of days and a lot of history.

I credit my chronic pain for the fact that I take very little for granted. For years, I have woken up and tried to appreciate what my body will allow me to do that day. I've learned to live in the moment, good or bad knowing it could be worse. I've tried to use this same outlook when things are not going well, thinking to myself, "Am I safe? Do I have my basic needs met? Are my kids safe?" Perspective - it's all about perspective, right?

As we stumble our way through this huge tragedy in our lives, Madi knows so many who have lost loved ones and have no home to go back to, no other family to surround them or talk to, and who fear for their own safety. Here, we are surrounded by the love of our friends and chosen family.

Both kids talk about how we didn't take our time together for granted. That we really got the very best out of the short time we had. What an incredible thing to be able to recognize and appreciate.

Yes, a chunk of our hearts is gone, and as painful as it is, life seems to continue to chug along. I have no idea how we are going to get through this next year without Jim. What I do know, is that we are going to do it together and that we are surrounded by the most amazing people. For now, it's one day at a time.

MAY 2, 2017 LINDA:

I find it unbelievable that as I go to write my feelings down, I stumble upon Madi post and she says exactly what I'm thinking and feeling. She beautifully expressed the exhaustion that has overcome our house this week.

I know I'm "resting" when I go to bed, but I feel far from rested when I drag my ass out of bed every morning. I know I have things to do, places to go, people to see. I fear people notice that I'm not "all" there when I show up.

I'm not ok with this "new normal". I'm not ok when things come up with the kids and I can't text or call Jim to discuss how we should approach things. I'm not ok being at the store and throwing something in the cart for Jim before realizing I don't need it. I'm not ok with counting Jim when I call to make reservations for dinner.

This business of grieving is exhausting and unpredictable. There is a heaviness to the environment here. Jim and my dad were two constants for most of my life. To have them physically gone feels empty. It's more than a void, it's an emptiness that can't be filled with anything else. The moments of joy I feel (and yes, there are moments of joy) don't add anything to this emptiness. The twice daily calls with my mom remind me that grief can have a cruel impact on one's brain, and yet also a reminder to embrace every "conversation" with her even if we go over the same things every time. What a gift it is to be able to still hear her voice.

And yet, there is perspective. It doesn't necessarily help with the emptiness, but I see little cracks of light that will grow bigger as time goes on, and with that light will come energy. I know that with this loss comes great responsibility to live life in a way that Jim and my dad would have wanted. Indeed, it was a great privilege to have had two such incredible people in my life in such an intimate way.

It's supposed to be 70 degrees on Thursday. I hope to feel the sun on my face a lot that day. I know so many people facing huge struggles and similar feelings of emptiness. My wish is to feel more light and that the fog that hangs over us lifts a bit.

May 2, 2017 Madi:

I am so, so, tired. I'm learning that this grieving process is a lot like my time in Greece. I'm attempting to normalize a situation that is abnormal, not fair, and really sad, because that's the only way that life can go on. I need to devise a routine in this new life to stay sane.

Thank god I have the wisdom from those experiences to know that as time passes, I begin to heal, even if right now it feels like I am constantly banging my head against a wall, falling into bed exhausted but unable to sleep, getting up every day and trying to kick ass but NEVER feeling accomplished or rested.

Grief just sucks it all out of you, it's really just a battle to keep filling up a bucket that's got a bunch of holes. The sadness will drain you, so it's a matter of pouring in enough happiness to keep from getting down to empty.

Grief is learning how to fill the void left behind when the only two men to ever love you unconditionally are suddenly gone. It's learning how to be strong enough for yourself and for those around you who are also feeling the empty space that such kind and encompassing souls leave behind.

Grief is my heart shattering a million times a day when I think of my precious friend Rezgar who was robbed of a childhood, my friend Yussef who will carry the psychological trauma of war with him for the rest of his life, my friend Robinson who is a paraplegic living in extreme poverty, suffering needlessly when everything he'd need to be rehabilitated is just a plane ride away yet inaccessible to him because of the geography of his birth.

Grief is heavy. This is a lot to carry, but not a burden. I consider it a great privilege to witness such strength and resilience in these people I have met and come to love. Their stories give me strength when I've needed it the most. They've shown me again and again what it's like to pick yourself up, dust yourself off, and get back on the horse. When I can't find the will to go on in myself, I find it in them. I consider myself the luckiest person alive to have received such gifts from people who were total strangers, and to receive the endless gift of love from my dad, from my grandpa, and from the community they thoughtfully surrounded me with before making their exits from this world. So grief is not a burden. It is far from it.

Grief is nearly an expression of emotion. It means that I loved something so much and so deeply that it hurts like hell to have it taken away. To be tired like this means that it energized me, it fueled my passion for the world, and to experience that, even just for a moment in your life, is truly a beautiful thing.

Winnowing

Donna James

The fridge is almost emptied of juices
and pickles. Sardines gone from the cupboard.
I have fed crows stale chips
from cellophane bags long past pull date.

Not a German sausage or potato in the house.
Greens from the farmers' market fill my bins.
Metaphors swept from my rooms,
slowly at first, as I wake up,
beginning with the easily dismissed.

Your razor tossed from the second drawer;
your robe hanging in the basement
with no place to go after last week's laundry.

Shirts thrown in the trunk of a car
headed to a homeless shelter, coat and gloves
shipped to Standing Rock for the winter.

Near the portal, the chakra Buddha sits,
incandescent on his rock above the CDs
from the days before you downloaded Spotify.

That painting of cosmic particles I finally love
stays where you hung it your first round of chemo;
it forms a canopy for my altar,

now hallowed with sympathy cards,
the wooden Ganesha I hand-carried from our dacha,
and a map to your grave in the meadow.

Our cat has crossed over to find you,
her bowls stowed in a bottom drawer.
For now, I travel without company.

I sleep naked, still. I read until I am too tired
to want your body, too sleepy to remember
it's no use waiting up for you.

What is it like to...?

Jeanne Broadbent
Katrina Taee

Introduction

The poem "What is it like to...?" began life during my PhD research into the impact of traumatic bereavement on therapists' personal and professional identity and practice (Broadbent, 2015).

One of my participants was Katrina Taee. In my interview with her, Katrina gave a powerful and moving chronicle of her experience of traumatic bereavement and grief, and described how this experience had affected her both personally and professionally as a therapist over a period of some years. During the process of immersing myself deeply in the analysis of Katrina's transcript, I was struck once again by the emotional intensity of her experience and her powerful descriptions of living through grief. As I engaged reflexively with her experience and listened many times to her 'voice', I felt a spontaneous desire to put Katrina's words into a form that would encapsulate the totality of her experience and so I created the poem. It uses Katrina's words as she spoke them in our interview, but I have placed them in a poetic form, using appropriate headings and repetitions. I believe the poem captures Katrina's unique response to the deaths of her parents, the effects of their deaths on her as a person, and the impact these experiences of grief and loss have had on her development as a therapist. The poem highlights that the experience of grief is unpredictable, changes over time, and cannot be truly 'known'. It also demonstrates that understanding, forgiveness and healing are also part of this ever-evolving process.

What is it like to...?

Prologue - Louise

What is it like to be a parentless child?
To be alone with your sister and not have your brother?
What is it like to be the eldest?
The head of the family,

The matriarch.
To give up a home you've lived in or known for fifty-four years.
To know you were one of five and now you are one of two?
A tiny unit in the universe.
These things I understand.

FATHER

What is it like to hear of your father's death just as you were
breathing out a sigh of relief?
What is it like to see your father's body and sit next to it?
To feel the anger and resentment and curiosity when his deceit is
revealed?
What is it like to try and understand your father as a person?

These things I understand.

MOTHER

What is it like to take over your father's role?
To parent your mother and keep her safe as she withdraws into
her own nocturnal world?
To feel anger that she's not grieving –'never said a word about it
not a word nothing never cried
nothing!'
To have no space for grief.
To feel the anger as your own grief is swamped by her ever-
increasing needs of care,
To have to check-on-her-check-house-do-shopping-cook-
meals-pay-bills-deal-with-gardeners-deal-with-probate-run-
everything ...
And to feel it eat into your life like a cancer...

What is it like to see your mother getting really sick in hospital
following her accident?
In a disgusting ward
And having horrible care
And having to go into a nursing home?
What is it like to see your mother dementing and declining?
To wipe her bottom and clean up her faeces?

To watch her shrink ... shrink her way out of the world?
To try to make sense of that?
What is it like to feel completely undone
by hearing the words "D'you know darling, I really do love you".
To feel her gently stroking your face,
To know that tenderness at the end,
To drop past hates and resentments.
To reconnect.

What is it like to spend a day with your mother's body
And wash her
And prepare her
And pluck the hair off her face
Because she's donated her body to medical science?
To not have a funeral for a year.
What is it like to feel overwhelming relief,
To no longer feel guilty,
To feel free,
To have your life back?

These things I understand.

GRIEF

What is it like to bear the burden of grief?
What is it like to have grief in your body?
To have legs of steel
To feel your body coming to a grinding halt
To just want to sleep
To feel a stultifying immobility in yourself to move forward in a
way you normally would?
To feel battered and bruised and very tender.
To feel a heaviness in your soul that seeps into your body ...
What is it like to know you haven't the strength or the energy or
the mind-set to hold your clients?
To know that you could not have listened to their stories and sepa-
rated it out from your own grief?
To know it would not have been safe
It absolutely would not have been safe for them.
These things I understand from my perspective.

INTEGRATION

What is it like to feel richer for having gone through one of life's huge transitions?
To know that it will be a life without your parents
To know that you're on a journey, a grief journey
That no two days will be the same
To know that you'll experience seismic shifts within.
What is it like to know that your work is informed by practical experience?
To feel that your experience opens your heart to empathy more than it was already opened.
To bring to your work three different experiences of bereavement?
To understand the subtleties and nuances of individual experience.
To feel richer
And wiser
And more empathic ...
To have no fear of death
To know you can listen and empathise with your clients
To feel like a magnet for death.

These things I understand ...

LEGACY

What is it like to spend a year sorting out thousands of photographs of my family from birth to death?
To lay out my brother's and my parents' lives
To really understand them,
To get that in my bones.
To feel them come closer to me as people?
To feel on a continuing journey with my parents...
And when the probate is done
And all the letters are done
And the house is cleared
And sold
And then there's this last thing, this photographic project ...
Then it's done .
Everything is done.
So I don't know what that bit's going to be like yet...
When it's all done.
Then it's just me and my sister and memories I guess...

CODA

And that will enrich my work as well because at some point for
everybody –
Even though we carry them with us –
But when the practicalities are done
You're left with just the things you remember that you love with
your emotions.

And these things I will also come to understand.

Reference: Broadbent, J.R. (2015), 'An Interpretative
Phenomenological Analysis of the lived experience of traumatic
bereavement on therapists' personal and professional identity and
practice. Unpublished PhD thesis.

THE WORN PATH OF MAY 7TH

Kimberly C Paul

Today I woke up feeling the hurricane of unbearable loss and grief. I want to push it away because tears should not fall eighteen years later, but they do. As I toss in my bed hoping this day will not come again, I watch the clock hit 7:43am. I turn over as I hear the hollow sounds of my German Shepherd walking toward my bed. I turn to see her sweet face encouraging me to rise.

The clock now reads 9:10am. I lay in my bed staring at the ceiling hoping that I'm still dreaming, but I am not. For this I know for sure, I can't think my way out of this heaviness... I have to act my way out. So, I sit up. I place my feet on the old hardwood floors and lean forward.

As I slowly grab the leash, Haven starts to stretch knowing that her walk is close at hand. I'm afraid to open the door to the outside world to expose my raw wounded soul to a world abandoned and seems to have no place for old grief. As I walk toward the park, it is overcast and strangely quiet this Monday morning. My motivation is weak as I feel the slight pull forward from the leash. As I approach the park, the grass is being mowed. The smell is fresh and renewed. It is here in nature I find the bravery to accept that grief is a journey that will never end. I look up at the tall 200 hundred-year-old trees swaying in the wind. I close my eyes and feel it on my face. I chuckle, knowing the fact that you can feel something without seeing it. It somehow opens my heart to the mysteries of life. This place, nature, is where I find peace. It is where I find him. I try to put my arms around this deep misunderstanding of life and death because it somehow is self-evident that all things in nature live and die. It is the cycle of life we human tend to avoid or acknowledge until it is too late, and the present moment has passed.

I toss the ball to a happy dog walking through the yet un-mowed area, eating talk grass, and smelling all types of natural happenings. My dog does not know it, but she is awakening me, teaching me to walk and act my way through this day. I suddenly look up and the wind blows through my hair. I raise my arms to the cloudy sky and ask for what I want. I don't ask for my grief to leave me, I ask for the guidance and the resources to learn to live and carry my grief well.

I ask for forgiveness. I ask for courage. I ask for strength.

I want to push away the unimaginable, but instead I lean into it knowing that all rebirths come with a little labor and pain. I turn my heart toward knowing this grief will ease, but never leave me. The center of this hurricane, of this grief, calms my soul once again. The next steps toward the unknown, I feel fear, not knowing what the future holds. I settle into my meditation spot in front of the fireplace, cross my legs and pray. As my eyes open, I take note of all these material items that make my home a home. I realize I don't need them anymore to feel complete.

The morning clouds are lifting making way to the beautiful blue skies peeking through to reminded me once again of heaviness will lift again too. It is in this moment, a tear falls, a goodbye is whispered and the only words that come are, "I'll see you soon. It is only a matter of time." I hate to see May 7 come and I hate to see it leave – but knowing the worn path will be walked again in an effort to prove that life is short, fragile and has an expiration date for all of us. So, we all must live with bold intentions.

Yet, this year seems different. This year, I know what I have to do. I hear the distant call of change. I pray for the resources I need to continue my life while carrying my grief with me every step of the way, but now celebrating the legacy, and memories that are now forming the person I've longed to be.

LIVING LOSS
CHOOSING HAPPINESS

Kathleen LaFrancis Eaton, PhD

"It's not okay," were the first and last words I gave Sierra, a courageous fellow author who asked me to sign her book. She'd read her essay poignantly and honestly. It was about rape by a friend, the ultimate betrayal. A girlfriend flew with her from far away to read, a healing and loving act. Both sisters in this violence of betrayal, we wept silently and hugged fiercely.

Sierra is twenty years younger than my daughter; she could be my granddaughter, yet we suffer the same pain. Part of me is jealous of her. There's a friend at her side who is willing to share her pain, who is willing to stand up to the world and bear witness to her experience.

In my day and age, there was no telling and sharing. Even with my mother, and no doubt Sierra's, there was no help, no solace. Though I sought help from my mother and the parish priest; no one believed me. Recently a friend, who I'd told at the time, recounted their feeling.

They had no way, then, to understand.

For most of my life, I grieved at every protective act a mother took for her child because none had been taken for me. I had no personal experience of it, except to watch my mother with my brother.

That is, until my daughter was born, and I promised her all I could give, and that nothing would ever hurt her. Now she has two boys of her own. I did my best; but she certainly has had enough suffering, regrettably some from my own history. The worst was that her father demanded full custody after our divorce. He'd sworn to prove me an unfit mother, because I'd been an abused child. I knew he'd do anything to accomplish that no matter how untrue. Our culture was not on the side of abused woman. I was not going to allow my daughter to be kidnapped and emotionally ripped apart by a custody battle. I knew all too well the feeling from the way my father had ripped my small body and heart apart. I could keep her whole by letting her go.

Undoubtedly, we are closer because I knew where she was. Her father's parents were good people and that's where he took her.

In that way, I was able to stay as close as possible under the circumstances. When she went to college, she came to live with me. Now we live close, we see each other often, and I enjoy my grandsons.

My grief included pain around motherhood, and for more than a decade simply being asked about having children brought anguish. It wasn't accepted that kids, especially a daughter, would live with their fathers. Never mind that. I missed her terribly. Then comes another Mother's Day, which is torture on wheels. Even my wonderful husband is perplexed as to what to do. Still, I immerse myself in a day of vigorous gardening to avoid the syrupy sentiments that go both up and down a generation making me uncomfortable.

Why then would I choose to write about this? Truly it is not for my own healing, that is accomplished, for the most part. Healing, for me, was a serious matter. I chose long ago to be happy. My daughter is now forty-four. We have good years to cherish, and we look forward to many more.

My father has passed away. The last time I saw him was a long, long time ago, some fifteen years before he died. At that time, he complained I hadn't given him proper attention when he graduated with his Masters' degree. Certainly, he wasn't a great correspondent and I knew little of his life. That didn't bother me. Yet, to my chagrin, he insisted on visiting me. This complaint topped it off. He'd not paid a dime for any of my degrees, nor even sent a congratulatory card. All of these demands continued. Such egocentrism after he'd treated me like his strumpet until I was strong enough to fight him off. That last visit, when I dropped him at the airport I said, "Don't come back until you feel like being a father." His response was, "What have I done to you lately?" This was the closest to an apology I'd ever get. Not a word came from him again! I was younger, then, than my daughter is now.

The situation for my mom couldn't have been good. I have forgiven her and told her so, though she now denies the conversations we've had. "Nothing like that ever happened." The exact response she gave the priest when he came to the house. It was no help at all. The best, for me, is minimal to no contact with my mother. It's just too painful.

Again, why do I write? It's for Sierra and all of my other sisters. I am happy and you can be too. Don't be afraid to make mistakes. The kind talked about here are not yours. And that such violence happened to you is not okay. You owe yourself a happier way. What happened wasn't your mistake; it was his. Find the path you want. Make a choice and don't look back, except to realize you are strong, intelligent, and beautiful from the inside out.

Namasté.

EVERYWHERE

Maureen Geraghty

The day comes
when the body sighs its heaviness
letting go, like a child would a balloon-
release and rest
where finally, after years of
love and struggle
the soul expands, like spores of a dandelion.
The day comes
when we who are left with our breath and bones,
liberate, like a tree dropping ripe fruit,
allow the one we love
to enter us in a new way
like paper into fire.
The day comes
when we realize death is not loss
like clouds that uncover sun
like coins in a shadow,
but instead notice our loved one
in our hands, in our children's eyes.
When this day comes
we stand together
and as a breeze animates the trees
the spirits of those passed
permeate our beings, inhabit new space within Life
And we begin to re-discover the beloved

Everywhere.

AUTHORS

KRISTINA ASHLEY has been interested in death, dying, and grief, since she was in her early twenties. She has had truly powerful experiences with clients doing past life regressions as a certified hypnotherapist. She always felt there was something beyond the physical body, and that the soul retains memory and lives on, building towards full realization of itself. Kristina's work as a caregiver has affirmed to her that the times of birth and death are truly the most powerful. Her book, *All Was Love*, helps change the way we think and feel about death, life and love. www.allwaslove.com

PAUL ATREIDES is a theatre critic and columnist for *EatMoreArtVegas.com*, and contributor to *Desert Companion*, a Nevada NPR/PBS publication. The *"World of Deadheads," Book 3, Nathan's Clan of Deadheads*, is the latest in his paranormal humor series; all three are available through Amazon. Current works in progress include *Of Monsters and Men* (working title), a novel about domestic violence, and *Sins of the Fathers*, a drama for the stage.
Visit his website: www.paul-atreides.com
Follow him on Twitter: @atreides_paul
Find him on Facebook: www.facebook.com/paul.atreides.391 and www.facebook.com/WorldofDeadheads

BETH RAHE BALAS, Grief Dialogues Advisory Council member and editor, fled from Philly to the Pacific Northwest 30 years ago with her husband. They built a home and raised their family on a little island halfway between the wild Olympic Peninsula and bustling Seattle. Her 2016 essay, "The Clan Stitch" can be found at www.stories.griefdialogues.com/2016/11/04/the-clan-stitch, and poem "Too Early Too Late" in the 2017 book *Just a Little More Time* and is an editor with Green Flash Books. A teacher and visual artist, she designs gardens, among other things.

PAUL BOARDMAN is a writer and interfaith Funeral Chaplain and Celebrant living in Seattle, Washington. He grew up in Tokyo, Japan, and holds the farcically-named "Masters of Divinity" from Princeton Theological Seminary. Two of his enduring thematic obsessions in writing are: what constitutes a good life in the face of death/loss and the nature of yearning, even greed, for love. His work has been featured in *The Good Men Project, Gravel, Thrive Global, P.S. I Love You, Veterans News Report,* and *ICCFA Magazine,* and in the anthologies *Just a Little More Time, We Came to Say* and *We Came Back to Say.* He is looking to place his memoir.

DR JEANNE BROADBENT is based in the North West region of the UK. She is an experienced humanistic therapist currently working with clients in a hospice and in private practice. Jeanne has a long-standing interest in issues of loss, bereavement and grief, and the uniqueness of this experience for the individual. She is particularly interested in traumatic bereavement and completed her PhD in this area in 2015.

DIANA BURBANO, a Colombian immigrant, is an Equity actor, a playwright and a teaching artist at South Coast Repertory and Breath of Fire Latina Theatre Ensemble.

Diana's plays focus on female protagonists and social issues. Written work includes *Policarpa, Fabulous Monsters, Caliban's Island, Enemy\Flint,* and *Linda,* (in English and in Spanish), which has been seen all over the world. As an actor she originated the roles of Ama de Casa in the Spanish version of *Menopause the Musical, Thumb in Imagine,* and Ana Guerrero in Jose Cruz Gonzales' *Long Road Today/El Largo Camino de Hoy* at South Coast Repertory. www.dianaburbano.com

JENNIFER COATES - When not practicing and writing about tax law, Jennifer Coates writes poetry. She finds writing about tax law and writing poetry oddly similar and similarly satisfying. For both, she has to sink into the more spacious layers of words, to express content that doesn't readily lend itself to easy expression-- to take something extremely abstract, like emotions and mood, or abstruse tax concepts, and somehow make the abstraction concrete. It's one of her favorite things to do. Jennifer's poetry has been included in several anthologies, including *Just a Little More Time,* the annual juried *Poetry Corners* celebration of displayed poetry on Bainbridge Island, Washington during National Poetry Month, and *Ars Poetica,* a yearly juried pairing of visual arts and poetry in Kitsap County, Washington. Jennifer is honored to be included in this collection. Jennifer came to the Pacific Northwest with her husband and daughter 12 years ago from the NYC metro area and has not looked back since.

ELIZABETH COPLAN is the founder of the non-profit Grief Dialogues, an artistic movement, to create a new conversation about dying, death, and grief, She is an award-winning playwright, educator, speaker, and subject matter curator who helps others explore their grief and attitudes toward death. Her recent film *8AM* won several awards for selection at the Seattle International Film Festival, Michael Moore's Traverse City Film Festival, Byron Bay Festival (Australia), Cleveland International Film Festival, and YES Film Festival in Columbus, IN. In summer 2018, her play, *Grief Dialogues*, enjoyed sold out performances in Seattle, and at the Dramatists Guild National Conference in New York. In fall 2018, Elizabeth took the play to Las Vegas to honor the victims/survivors/first responders and good samaritans of the October 1, 2017 mass shooting. In October 2018 the film version of the play is scheduled during ReimagineNYC, a week long event in New York to explore life and death. www.griefdialogues.com

MIKE CORDLE is a writer living in the Pacific Northwest. He was in the ministry for over 20 years. Now he works at a facility for people with dementia. He has had some of his work published in *Manastash*, the literary art journal of Central Washington University, his alma mater, as well as in the online magazine and blog *Killing the Buddha*.

ASPEN DRAKE is 22 years old and has three younger siblings. They lost our mother to breast cancer in the early spring of 2016. Aspen now publishes a podcast titled *Loss For Words*, in hopes to document their grief journey for others who are on theirs.

KATHLEEN LaFRANCIS EATON is an award-winning author. Her works include essays, gardening articles, fiction and traditional murder mysteries. She has been a nurse, a consultant, and a CEO. Grief, she has learned, informs us of our great love of life and of each other. Fear not to love, fear not to grieve, it shows our humanity. Grief is the greatest of caring as it outlives the beloved and caries their gifts to others empowering others to carry on their work. www.KathleenEaton.net

ALISON ECKELS writes with a group at Cancer Lifeline in Seattle and on her own. Her father was an old-fashioned family doctor. His dinner table stories made clear that death is a part of life, as much as birth and all the years in between. Alison attended a Quaker school where they spoke of the Inner Light in all of us. Later she found a meditation group which taught that we are that light within, and our bodies are our home for each lifetime.

SHARON EHLERS is the author of *Grief Reiki®- An Integrated Approach to the Emotional, Physical and Spiritual Components of Grief and Loss*. She is co-author of *Grief Diaries: Surviving Loss by Suicide* which was a three-time finalist in the 10th Annual National Indie Excellence Awards, the 2016 Book Excellence Awards and the 2016 Best Book Awards. She is also a contributor to other books in the Grief Diaries anthology including *Hello from Heaven, How to Help the Newly Bereaved, Grieving for the Living and Loss of a Loved One*. Sharon was recently named an expert instructor with the International Grief Institute. Her best lesson in life is: "Miracles do happen."

AMY FERRIS is an author, editor, screenwriter & playwright. Her memoir, *Marrying George Clooney, Confessions From A Midlife Crisis* (Seal Press, 2010) was adapted into an Off-Broadway play. She has written for both TV and film. Her screenplay, *Funny Valentines*, was nominated for a Best Screenplay award (BET) in 2000. She is the co-editor of the anthology, *Dancing at The Shame Prom* (Seal Press, 2012) and most recently editor of Shades Of Blue, Writers on Depression, Suicide, and Feeling Blue (Seal Press, 2015). Amy was recently named - and awarded - one of Women's eNews 2018 21 LEADERS FOR THE 21ST CENTURY. She is currently writing the book for the play/musical *#MeToo the Musical*. You can read her blog at www.marryinggeorgeclooney.com

ALICA FORNERET is a creative exploring death, dying, and grief through storytelling. With over 10 years of experience as an editor and writer, Alica's work has taken her all over the world—she's eaten, written, and traveled her way across Europe, the United Kingdom, the United States, Canada, Mexico, and Australia. She now works with an extensive network of international writers and artists as collaborative partners for print and digital death-focused projects. www.alicaforneret.com

ROBYN FAUST GABE decided to take her pain combined with multiple losses to benefit other bereaved siblings. In 2010, she enrolled in a doctoral program at Nova Southeastern. There she studied sibling bereavement issues utilizing theoretical lenses associated with the conflict analysis and resolution field. In 2016, Dr. Gabe graduated with her PhD.

MAUREEN GERAGHTY has been teaching high school for over 27 years, mostly in alternative school settings. She is the mother of two fantastic children. Maureen has published a book of poems entitled, *Look Up-Poems of a Life*. Her poems, essays, and stories are published by *The National Writing Project, Re-Thinking Schools, Watch My Rising Anthology, Tacenda Literary Journal, mamazine.com, Teaching with Heart, Mothering.com* and most recently she published a children's book, *Grandpa Ron's Bird Food*. She lives in Portland, Oregon.

SARA J GLERUM - After fifty-two years of marriage, Sara J. Glerum is reinventing herself as a widow. To keep in contact with her far-flung offspring and families, she writes a blog, *Beats Talking To Myself*. She has received recognition in several writing contests, and dozens of her of personal essays have been published.

EMMA GOLDMAN-SHERMAN's plays include w*hy birds fly, Abraham's Daughters*, and *WHORTICULTURE*, all named semi-finalists for *Risk Is This Festival* at Cutting Ball (2014, 2015, and 2017). *Perfect Women* won a Jane Chambers Award (produced by All Out Arts in New York and Theatre Conspiracy in Washington DC). Other productions include *Significant Circus* (Manhattan Theatre Source), *Wombshot* (Circle Rep Lab, Take One Prods. at Camilla's and The Culture Project; at Grand Arts Gallery in Kansas City; and at Canal Cafe Theatre in London). *Counting in Sha'ab* was produced by Golden Thread in the ReOrient Festival of plays about the Middle East. Emma received residencies at The Millay Colony for the Arts, Ragdale, and twice at WordBridge where she returned as a dramaturg. She earned an MFA from the University of Iowa where Antigone's Sister won the Maibaum Award for plays addressing social justice. She is the Resident Dramaturg at the 29th Street Playwrights Collective where she runs the Write Now Workshop for new play development in NYC. Member: New Circle Theatre Company, LPTW, and the Dramatists Guild.

GWEN GOODKIN's writing has been published by Fiction, Witness, The Dublin Review, The Carolina Quarterly, Atticus Review, jmww, Exposition Review, The Rumpus, Reed Magazine and others. She has twice been nominated for a Pushcart Prize and has won the Black Fox Literary Magazine Contest as well as the John Steinbeck Award for Fiction. She also writes for the screen and stage. Her website is www.gwengoodkin.com

Rachel Greenberg's life changed in an instant on March 23, 2013. While she was out doing Saturday errands, her husband Glenn suffered a fatal brain hemorrhage. They never spoke to each other again. She was thrown into this thing called "grief" and had no idea what to do.

In 2017, she started Connections of Hope where she helps the bereaved to know they are not alone in their grief. She has been a guest on several international podcasts, she is active on social media, @ConnectionsHope, and is a regular public speaker in Southern California on all things grief, death, dying and hope. She is currently writing a memoir, "Finding Glenn." She lives in Hermosa Beach, CA.

Erin Harrop is a medical social worker and third year doctoral student at the University of Washington School of Social Work. Her research focuses on eating disorders, stigma, and chronic illness. In her free time, she enjoys spending time with her family, playing outside, and creating things.

Linda Shadwell Hart and her husband Greg were married in 1989 and have two children, Allison and Spencer. Greg was an architect and a principal in a Seattle firm. His passion was building environmentally sound schools. Linda retired from a career of emergency room nursing once Greg quit work. She has helped ease many people into death in a clinical setting. "I could never have foreseen what I experienced in the comfort of my own home. Praying that each breath would be my husband's last, and left to struggle through a process that while legal, offered only a 'one size fits all' tool."

Donna James is a psychotherapist in private practice in Seattle. She began writing poetry and essays shortly before her husband's cancer diagnosis, allowing her to write her way through his treatment and death, and through her own grief. Her current work touches on relationship, science, the state of our world, aging, and visual art.

Susan Johnson spent a forty year career in advocacy and health policy at the state and national levels culminating in an appointment by President Barack Obama to serve as Health and Human Services Director of Region 10. Now retired, she enjoys fly fishing, watercolor painting, skiing, golf, tennis, pickleball and travel.

Kara LC Jones is the Creative Grief Educator and heARTist behind GriefAndCreativity.com. She co-founded both the Creative

Grief Studio and KotaPress. She's a Carnegie Mellon graduate who interned 3 years at *Mister Rogers Neighborhood* back in the day.

Toni Lepeska's diverse career in journalism spans 29 years of writing about criminal justice, community development, and business growth. Based in Memphis, Tennessee, she currently is a freelance writer and editor. An aspiring author, she blogs about her personal journey of healing and the transformative impact of grief at www.tonilepeska.com.

Ann Lovejoy is the author of numerous books on gardening, garden design, and sustainable gardening. Ann has also written several cookbooks, including *Cooking At Harmony Hill*, which supports free workshops and retreats for people affected by cancer. For over 20 years, she has led the Friday Tidy volunteers in caring for award winning gardens at the Bainbridge Public library. In recent years, Ann has designed and planted several public landscapes, including the gardens at Waypoint Park and Hannah's Garden at Owen's Playground, an accessible play space for people of all ages and abilities. Her current projects include Transfriending, a support group for family and friends of people in or considering gender transition, and the Peace Cafe, open community conversations on challenging topics such as hope, affordable housing, gun control and school safety. She lives on Bainbridge Island, where she is active in promoting affordable housing.

Mary McLaughlin is a pen name. The writer chooses to remain anonymous.

Florrie Munat is the author of *Be Brave: A Wife's Journey Through Caregiving* (2017), a memoir about her forty-year marriage, focusing on the years she was a caregiver for her husband Chuck who had Lewy body dementia. Florrie is the author of several children's books, articles, stories and YA book reviews. She's also been a reference librarian, English teacher, and university press worker. Learn more about Florrie and Be Brave at www.florriemunat.com.

Dr Robert A Neimeyer is Psychology Professor at University of Memphis and Director of The Portland Institute for Loss and Transition, and Board Member of Grief Dialogues. "Our connections define us, and we can accomplish far more together than we can independently." His book, *The Art of Longing: Selected Poems, 2009*, was published by BookSurge Publishing and can be purchased through Amazon online.

Toti O'Brien is the Italian Accordionist with the Irish Last Name. She was born in Rome then moved to Los Angeles, where she makes a living as a self-employed artist, performing musician and professional dancer. Her work has most recently appeared in *Heavy Feather, Triggerfish, The Almagre Review*, and *O:JA&L*.

Kimberly C Paul is a lifelong storyteller who wants to radically change the way people face end of life. From the set of Saturday Night Live to casting for CBS daytime, Kimberly has a passion for connecting with audiences. She has spent the last 17 years telling a very different kind of story. As VP of Outreach and Communications for a Wilmington, NC hospice, she created award-winning marketing strategies to share stories of how hospice patients and their loved ones face the end of life journey, and the keys to making every moment matter. Author, Host of *Death by Design Podcast*, and a Ted X Talk Speaker, her newest book, *Bridging The Gap*, hopes to change how people talk, design and plan for their own end of life. Bring the *Live Well Die Well Tour* to your town or city. www.livewelldiewelltour.com

Vanessa Poster, a member of the Los Angeles Poets and Writer's Collective, studied Method Writing with Jack Grapes for more than 20 years and is part of the Poetry Salon since 2017. Her work appears in literary publications including *Thieving Magpie, ONTHEBUS, I'll have Wednesday, and Fourth & Sycamore*. She is a writing coach and runs the writing workshop: "The Write Way: Using the Written Word to Heal Grief." Vanessa is a graduate of Stanford University with a Bachelors in Humanities and a Masters in Modern Thought and Literature. Widowed in 2015, Vanessa writes poems exploring themes of grief, love and gratitude. Both poems appearing in this volume, "We Danced," and "Stages of Grief," were previously published in the *Thieving Magpie*.

Richard Rosario is a native of Fox River Grove, Illinois. He is retired from the practice of law in Illinois and teaching public school in Las Vegas, Nevada. He currently resides in Las Vegas, Nevada with his wife and adult children. He has self-published two novels, *Burned Out: Confessions of a Public School Teacher* and *Doubting Thomas*, as well as a book of biblical satirical plays, *The Silliest Story Ever Told*. All three works are available on Amazon.

AIMEE ROSS is a nationally award-winning educator who has been a high school English teacher for the past twenty-five years and who will publish *Permanent Marker: A Memoir* in March 2018. She completed her MFA in Creative Non-Fiction Writing at Ashland University in 2014, and her writing has been published on lifein10minutes.com and SixHens.com, as well as in *Beauty around the World: A Cultural Encyclopedia, Scars: An Anthology, Today I Made a Difference: A Collection of Inspirational Stories from America's Top Educators*, and *Teaching Tolerance* magazine. Learn more at aimeerossblog.wordpress.com.

WILL SILVERMAN began writing poetry at age 12. Despite working a variety of jobs and various "career" paths, Will has consistently returned to writing as an outlet for his soul. In poetry, he enjoys the challenge of evoking emotions using strong, descriptive words in an efficient manner. Will spent his early years on the east coast, but finally found home in Montana. Drawing inspiration from mountains, Will spent 40 years in Missoula searching for passion in the beauty of his surroundings. Will derives his greatest inspiration from his children, Malia and Koby. Through them comes light, love and tremendous joy.

KATRINA TAEE lives and works in the UK. She was a Psychosynthesis counsellor for 18 years and had a private practice. Katrina also worked as a volunteer counsellor in a hospice with patients and families. She has always been interested in death, dying, grief and bereavement. Katrina Taee is now an End of Life Doula.

MARY LANGER THOMPSON's poems, short stories, and essays appear in various journals and anthologies. She is a contributor to two poetry writing texts, *The Working Poet* (Autumn Press, 2009) and *Women and Poetry: Writing, Revising, Publishing and Teaching* (McFarland, 2012), and was the 2012 Senior Poet Laureate of California. A retired school principal and former secondary English teacher, Langer Thompson received her Ed.D. from the University of California, Los Angeles. She enjoys conducting poetry workshops for schools, prisons, and in her community.

MEGAN VERED holds an MFA in Creative Writing from Vermont College of Fine Arts. Her work can be found in the *San Francisco Chronicle, Lake Effect, Silk Road Review*, and the *Mill Valley Historical Society Review*. She was a featured essayist in *Mezzo Cammin* and

Fifty Over Fifty Anthology. Her first-person writing focuses on family, friendship, faith, and the sounds of her youth.

DR JANE WILLIAMS is a clinical psychologist who has worked for over 25 years with individuals who have experienced trauma, life threatening illnesses, and grief. She completed a postdoctoral fellowship at Harvard Medical School where she trained in Medical Crisis Counseling. Dr. Williams has helped develop grief programs, made national presentations at grief conferences, and published peer-reviewed articles on grief. Her book, *Mysterious Moments: Thoughts That Transform Grief,* was recently published by Library Partners Press and can be purchased through Amazon and Barnes and Noble online, or in local independent bookstores. Dr. Williams recently retired from Wake Forest University Medical School.

JOCELYN WILLIAMS was born and raised in the San Francisco Bay Area. The first major loss she experienced was the death of her mother in 2002. Years later, she went on to get certified to teach Grief Recovery and now Jocelyn Williams is a trainer for the Grief Recovery Institute. "I began blogging as a single person in my 40's who had never been married because I recognized that I and many of my single friends experienced being single as a loss. So I started to blog about experienced related to that. And now I blog about a few more topics with a grief recovery perspective." www.mobettajo.com

TESS WILLIAMS is a pen name. The writer chooses to remain anonymous.

LINDA YASUTAKE and MADI WILLIAMSON are a mother and daughter who lost Linda's dad (Madi's Grandpa) and Madi's Papa, Jim (Linda's ex-husband and best friend) exactly three months apart. Linda trained as a social worker and is currently a volunteer soccer coach and soccer community advocate. Madi is working towards her Associates in Nursing and has spent three months in Greece working as a medical coordinator and advocate in the refugee camps. She has also spent time in the Dominican Republic on medical missions. She has a passion for reading, writing and traveling. A year after losing Jim, Linda lost her mom (Madi's grandma). Madi and Linda firmly believe that with great loss comes great love.

Resources

After Talk and Ask Dr. Neimeyer

Our Ask Dr. Neimeyer column is where renowned Grief Expert Dr. Robert Neimeyer answers reader's questions about grieving as well as anticipatory grief. And in our Resource Center you'll find books, DVDs and grief counseling resources for guidance and healing along with information-related financial, insurance and estate planning. After Talk – Online Grief Support – Because when a loved one leaves us, the grief can be overwhelming.

Sometimes, the sudden "aloneness" is too much to bear. The conversations throughout the day with a spouse, the phone calls or emails with a friend or child—never again. The silence is almost unendurable. You yearn to continue the conversation. If you are coping with grief, you've come to the right place. Our online grief support site offers grief blogs, inspirational quotes, and interactive writing tools to help you manage your grief. www.aftertalk.com

Charter for Compassion International

Charter for Compassion International provides an umbrella for people to engage in collaborative partnerships worldwide. Their mission is to bring to life the principles articulated in the Charter for Compassion through concrete, practical action in a myriad of sectors. Grief Dialogues is proud to be an Arts Partner of the Charter for Compassion.

Charter for Compassion
PO Box 10787
Bainbridge Island, WA 98110

www.charterforcompassion.org
Twitter: @TheCharter
Facebook: /CharterforCompassion
Instagram: /charterforcompassion
Join to make compassion a clear, luminous and dynamic force in our polarized world. Embrace the compassion revolution.

DEATH BY DESIGN PODCAST

Death by Design podcasts share interviews with hospice and pallia-tive care experts, authors, and artists. You will hear personal stories of caregivers inspired to create tools to help others with their own end of life journey as well as share intimate stories of those facing a serious illness. By sharing these stories and information, we hope you will learn how to design, plan and embrace your own end of life.

Host and death expert, Kimberly C. Paul, wants to radically change the way people face end of life, and she's using her extensive experi-ence as a storyteller to do just that. From the set of *Saturday Night Live* in New York City, to casting for CBS daytime, Kimberly has spent the last 17 years telling a very different kind of story. As Vice President of Outreach and Communications for Lower Cape Fear Hospice, she used a myriad of award-winning marketing strategies to share real stories about death and dying and the keys to making every moment matter.

Listen to her podcasts at www.deathbydesign.com/podcast. Her book *Bridging the Gap: Life Lessons from the Dying* is an innovative and uplifting book that invites the reader to move beyond the current standards of what death has come to mean in our culture. *Bridging the Gap* will empower you to design your death so it reflects your values, likes and dislikes and your personality. Death is not a final destination but a transcendental beginning. You can purchase the book from her website.

www.deathbydesign.com
Twitter: @kimberlypaulnc
Facebook: /deathbydesignpodcast

DEATH WITH DIGNITY

Death with Dignity National Center is a 501(c)3, nonpartisan, non-profit organization working to provide Death with Dignity as an option for dying individuals and to stimulate nationwide improve-ments in end-of-life care. The organization authored, passed, and defended the Oregon Death with Dignity Act (1994/1997/2006); was instrumental in passing the Washington (2008) Vermont (2013), and

California (2015) laws, and spearheaded the Maine (2000), Hawaii (2002), and Massachusetts (2012) campaigns.

www.DeathwithDignity.org
Twitter: @DeathwDignity
Facebook: /DeathwithDignity.

ELISABETH KUBLER-ROSS FOUNDATION

Dr. Elisabeth Kubler-Ross, author of the groundbreaking book, *On Death and Dying*, published 24 books during her lifetime, and has been translated into 34 languages. In her expansive body of work, she discussed care and support for the seriously ill, their families, the grieving and all who struggle with the effects of loss.

The Foundation participates in initiatives and collaborates with individuals and/or organizations that:

- Enhance compassionate care for the seriously ill and/or the dying
- Further the acceptance of death as a part of life (versus those that see death as a separate event apart from life)
- Enhance end-of-life care for special populations (such as those involved in hospice or palliative care for children, within the prison environment, or those living in remote populations or in developing countries, etc.
- Improve access to properly prescribed pain management medications as part of the end of life process
- Enhance communication surrounding all aspects of end of life care and compassionate care of the dying (and those that love them)
- Foster awareness of the power of love and forgiveness as an important component of one's life journey
- Enhance compassion and understanding of those who are grieving regardless of cause or origin
- Further the wishes of the end of life patient while respecting his or her right to humane treatment and compassionate care

www.ekrfoundation.org
Twitter: @KublerRoss
Facebook: /ekublerross

The Karuna Cards

Author and counselor Claudia Coenen created the Karuna Cards to offer creative ideas and activities for grief and other difficult life transitions. The cards encourage journaling, storytelling, collage and other ways to express grief and cope with troubling circumstances.

Use the Karuna Cards alone, or use them with family members, friends, or in counseling sessions.

Shattered by Grief: Picking up the pieces to become WHOLE again, written by Claudia Coenen, is a practical guide to help readers work through their grief via expressive therapies and activities, based on the techniques Claudia Coenen honed as a professional counselor after the unexpected loss of her husband. Find the book on Amazon and use Amazon Smile to make a donation to Grief Dialogues as part of your purchase.

www.thekarunaproject.com
Twitter: @cjkaruna
Facebook: /TheKarunaProject

Order of the Good Death

The Order of the Good Death is a group of funeral industry professionals, academics, and artists exploring ways to prepare a death phobic culture for their inevitable mortality.

If you are interested in learning more about the alternative death industry, visit their home funeral and natural burial pages for more information and links.

www.orderofthegooddeath.com
Twitter: @OrderGoodDeath
Facebook: /OrderoftheGoodDeath

SolaceClub, LLC

SolaceClub offers care packages for those in grief. Each SolaceClub box is psychologist-curated and designed to help those in grief cope with their symptoms. SolaceClub, LLC is dedicated to improving how we support those in grief. On the company's website, there are blogs devoted to ways in which people can better support the grieving as well as blogs written directly for those dealing with loss. SolaceClub, LLC also sponsors a monthly program which focuses on grief called SolaceShow (www.wcobm.tv). For more information, please go to www.solaceclub.com.

Speaking of Dying

Speaking of Dying offers a 30-minute film shines a gentle, bright light on dying and opens conversations about resources and planning. Screenings with presentation and Q & A are currently available throughout the Puget Sound area.

Speaking of Dying Workshops - Facilitated 4-session workshops engage participants in the challenges and resources necessary to plan for a peaceful and meaningful death. In the process they become comfortable speaking openly about their own wishes.

Call 206 985 0400 or email speakingofdying@speakingofdying.com for a schedule of fees.

ww.speakingofdying.com

About the Publisher

Grief Dialogues is an artistic movement, using theatre, visual art, film, music, podcasts, poetry, and narrative to start a new, safe conversation about dying, death, and grief. Sharing through art allows an immersion into the world of death and grief, breaking down old stigmas around these topics. We give voice to individual grief experiences and to the organizations/professions who help people in the process of dying and/or dealing with grief.

Grief Dialogues is dedicated to publishing books and materials that spark changes to our existing assumptions and expectations about death and grief. We believe in the fundamental right of all individuals to assert their personal dominion over illness and dying and how they grieve.

Elizabeth Coplan, Editor-in-Chief, believes people want to talk and write about their loss and their own fear of death... even those who never spoke of their grief before. The proof of this theory is found on the pages of this book.

Grief Dialogues also produces plays, films, art projects, podcasts, music and a website of resources.

www.griefdialogues.com
Twitter: @GriefDialogues
Facebook: /griefdialogues
Instagram: /griefdialogues

#OutofGriefComesArt

GRIEF DIALOGUES: THE PLAY

Grief Dialogues is a riveting set of short plays & poems created to end the stigma surrounding dying, death, and grief. Performances of *Grief Dialogues* encourage conversation, understanding, compassion, and empathy.

Interested in bringing "Grief Dialogues: The Play" to your town?
Visit: http://bit.ly/GDThePlay

8AM: A GRIEF DIALOGUES FILM

Adapted from the play *LA 8AM* by Mark Harvey Levine, 8AM is an award-winning short film that inspires the conversation between family healthcare providers, students, and therapists.

A thought-provoking film that prepares us for the moment before everything changes - when somebody dies.

Interested in a screening?
Visit: http://bit.ly/GDTheFilm

SPEAKING ENGAGEMENTS

Looking for an engaging speaker for your next event? Elizabeth Coplan is available worldwide to speak on "Using Theatre to Start the Conversation about Dying, Death, and Grief."

For more information please visit:
http://bit.ly/GDTheSpeaking

MORE FROM THE GRIEF DIALOGUES

The Art: http://bit.ly/GDTheArt
The Podcasts: http://bit.ly/GDThePodcasts
The Speaking: http://bit.ly/GDTheSpeaking
The Partners: http://bit.ly/GDOurPartners

CPSIA information can be obtained
at www.ICGtesting.com
Printed in the USA
LVHW012336200219
608286LV00006B/274/P